Thank
You so much
for your readership!
all my best,
:) K Cole

BOOKS BY KRESLEY COLE

The Immortals After Dark Series

The Warlord Wants Forever
A Hunger Like No Other
No Rest for the Wicked
Wicked Deeds on a Winter's Night
Dark Needs at Night's Edge
Dark Desires After Dusk
Kiss of a Demon King
Deep Kiss of Winter
Pleasure of a Dark Prince
Demon from the Dark
Dreams of a Dark Warrior
Lothaire
Shadow's Claim
MacRieve
Dark Skye
Sweet Ruin
Shadow's Seduction
Wicked Abyss
Munro

The Game Maker Series

The Professional
The Master
The Player

The Arcana Chronicles

Poison Princess
Endless Knight
Dead of Winter
Day Zero
Arcana Rsing
The Dark Calling
From the Grave

The MacCarrick Brothers Series

If You Dare
If You Desire
If You Deceive

The Sutherland Series

The Captain
The Price

KRESLEY COLE

THE
WITCH QUEEN
OF
HALLOWEEN

VALKYRIE PRESS
New York • Raven's Murk • Nightside • New Orleans

Valkyrie Press
228 Park Ave S #11599
New York, NY 10003

ISBN 979-8-9893762-1-6
ISBN 979-8-9893762-2-3
ISBN 979-8-9893762-0-9 (ebook)
Published in the United States of America.

Dedicated to Naomi—social media goddess, genuinely lovely person, and *force de la nature*—with all my heartfelt gratitude.

Dear Reader,

Before I discovered romance novels, I was mainly a fan of the horror genre, and I still love scary books and movies. Halloween—a celebration of costumes, candy, chills, and campy thrills—remains my favorite holiday.

So I thought I'd write a spicy romp about Halloween in the Lore, featuring one of the IAD's most notorious demon bachelors and his bold witch heroine. I had so much fun threading spooky Easter eggs throughout their love story and hope you enjoy!

Warmest,
:)kc

EXCERPTED FROM
THE LIVING BOOK OF LORE . . .

The Lore
". . . and those sentient creatures that are not mortal shall secretly coexist with humankind."

- Made up of immortals who can regenerate from most injuries.

The Demonarchies
"The demons are as varied as the bands of humankind. . . ."

- A collection of hundreds of demon dynasties.
- Most demons can teleport—or trace—and each breed has unique powers and vulnerabilities.
- A male demon must have intercourse with a potential mate to ascertain if she's his fated one—a process known as *attempting*.

The House of Witches
"Possessors of magical talents, practitioners of good and evil."

- Mystical mercenaries who sell their spells.
- Separated into five power castes: warrior, healer, enchantress, conjurer, and seeress.

The Ghouls

"Even immortals beware a ghoul's bite."

- Savage, undead monsters, with glowing green skin and yellow eyes.
- They live only to increase their number through their contagious bites and scratches.

The Møriør

"In the tongue of the Elserealms, Møriør can mean both 'the Dozen' and 'Soul's Doom.'"

- A sinister alliance of otherworldly beings.
- Have journeyed from the Elserealms to conquer the Lore.

The Accession

"And a time shall come when all immortals must fight and destroy each other."

- A mystical checks-and-balances system for an ever-growing population of Loreans.
- Occurs every five hundred years. Or right now . . .

THE
WITCH QUEEN
OF
HALLOWEEN

Fuck, fight, and revel: the life of a demon.

—RÖK KOURS, SMOKE DEMON,
SOLDIER OF FORTUNE, BETWEEN JOBS

Magic is a lover who won't be true.

—POPPY DYER, MERCENARY OF THE WICCAE,
CONCOCTIONESS, CURSED

PROLOGUE

New Orleans
Halloween

A priestess, a sorceress, and a Valkyrie meet in a graveyard," Nïx the Ever-Knowing said to her two visitors when they joined her atop a mausoleum roof. "I can't remember the punchline. Is it . . . *sex?*"

Bertil, the bat she carried on her shoulder, flapped his little wings. *Bat laughter.*

Loa the voodoo priestess sighed at Nïx's appearance. The Valkyrie soothsayer wore a plastic Viking hat with one horn missing, a pair of bell-bottoms, and no shoes or shirt. Two thick braids covered her breasts, the jet-black plaits gleaming in the waning light of the day.

From a distance, a Lykae's howl sounded, and thunder rumbled in waves. This Halloween would prove a night ripe for fate.

"The spirits told me you were here, Valkyrie," Loa said, her accent tinged with notes of a warm island paradise. "You're looking a fright." If Nïx was a fright, the priestess was a sight—dressed in a red number with a slit up the thigh to show off her knee-high boots. "Are you well?"

"I'm doing better than the Queen of Evil." Nïx hiked a

thumb at La Dorada. "She almost lost her life to a human last year, and it set back all of her regeneration."

"An unfounded rumor," Dorada said, though her life actually had been in jeopardy. With a nonchalant air, she smoothed her long, black mane and gold dust trickled down. Her mystical ring, one that granted wishes (with a catch), glinted in the last rays of the sun.

Nïx asked her, "And how did you find me, Dorada?"

"Only because you wanted to be found," she answered, her speech vibrating from a translator spell. "Something wicked rises, Valkyrie. Almost as wicked as I, and I walk in apocalypse." She didn't walk alone. Several of her undead Wendigos prowled among the crypts below, licking their lips for the taste of fresh corpses.

Loa cast an annoyed glance at the sorceress. The two weren't fans of each other. For one thing, like many in the Lore, Loa owed a debt to her—because of a granted wish—and no one knew when Dorada would collect on those debts.

For another, the sorceress's recent rising after centuries of mummification did in fact herald the end of this mortal realm.

Apocalypse . . . *soon*?

It didn't help that Dorada was a prickly sort of evil. Or, as Loa put it: "That sorceress woke on the wrong side of the sarcophagus."

So, naturally, Loa plotted to assassinate her. But what was a touch of murder between colleagues?

Now Loa told Nïx, "If we've been feeling this disturbance, you must have. Mariketa the Awaited dispatched someone on a mission tonight, and the fallout could be catastrophic. We feel the change coming. Is it already too late?"

"A disturbance in the Lore! Or is it the Lorce?" Nïx chuckled. So did Bertil. *Flap flap* went his wings.

Dorada glared. "I thought you had control over the House of Witches." Gaze going distant, she mused, "*I* could control them, if more of them were evil." She could compel any evil creature, enslaving them to her bidding.

Feigning a serious look, Nïx said, "We should address your shared worries head-on." She strolled over to a sunken area on the mausoleum roof, and the others followed. Kneeling in front of a puddle of water collecting there, she said, "Witch in the glass, come in. Witch in the glass, do you copy?"

Mariketa, a captromancer also known as the Queen of Reflections, was a young witch of unbelievable power. One could contact her through a reflection (unless she was in bed with her werewolf, which she often was).

"Breaker, breaker one-nine." Nïx grinned coyly at her audience of two Loreans and one bat. *Flap flap.* "Witch, come in?" Her reflection in the puddle clouded . . .

. . . and Mariketa's face took its place. "'Sup, Valkyrie? What a surprise!" The witch's expression—all innocent gray eyes—might have struck a three-millennia-old soothsayer as *rehearsed.*

"I have Dorada and Loa with me, and they've raised concerns on this Hallowed Eve."

"A meeting of alpha bitches?" Mari sounded hurt. "I could be there in a flash."

Nïx laughed. "Consider yourself safer there! Some of us atop this roof are mentally unwell. I do so worry about them."

Her companions looked bemused. Mari pointed toward Nïx's hat to say something, then clearly thought better of it.

"Spill, favorite Wiccan-type person," Nïx said. "Are you playing at fate tonight? Using some of your vast array of talents to see the future, perhaps?"

Mari's gaze darted. "You, uh, told me to use my powers for

good. This could change a lot."

In a scandalized tone, Nïx said, "This could change *everything*. Even monsters and mayhem have a purpose. Shouldn't you consult the coach before taking players off the bench?"

Dorada said, "The scales were balanced, and soon they won't be. It's too unpredictable. Even I can't compel so many."

Mari shook her head. "The scales weren't balanced as long as the Møriør have us in their sights."

The three fell silent at that. The Møriør was an alliance made up of primordials, each of them the oldest and most powerful being of a particular species.

Mari sighed. "Though Nïx won't cop to it, we all know they're favored to win this Accession."

"May the Lorce be with you!" Nïx exclaimed. When she rubbed her nose against Bertil's, the bat gazed up at her with dreamy adoration.

Dorada glowered at the Valkyrie. "If immortals consider a madwoman like you their leader—their *coach*—then maybe the Møriør should win." She waved to indicate Loa. "The priestess must think so, else she wouldn't be selling them information."

Loa's amber eyes glittered. "I'd watch your rottin' tongue, sorceress."

"It's no longer rotting!"

"Hey!" Mari cried. "Can we have just *one* discussion without arguing and imminent bloodshed?"

Dorada and Loa: *"NO!"*

"The journal," Nïx whispered, cutting through the tension. Her gaze had gone vacant. "The Enemy of Old is going to want it. Should I give it to him? Will anything matter after this?" Lightning flashed above. "The spheres are smudged once more. Will they crack under the pressure?"

The others grew uneasy, even Dorada.

Mari cleared her throat. "Uh, you okay there, Nïx?"

"*We* are not." She abruptly stood, telling Mari, "The die is cast. It's too late to change anything. Depending on what is unleashed tonight, the Lore will convulse. I hope you know what you're doing, because for once, I don't."

Mari swallowed. "That sounds less than ducky. I thought you'd still be acting as, like, the guardrails for me."

Dorada smirked. "Looks like you're about to careen off the cliff and take all of us with you."

Nïx didn't deny it. "That's the thing about shaping fate, young witch." She stomped her bare foot into the puddle; lightning flashed again, and water splattered up to her face. "Sometimes it *resists*." The bat didn't laugh when droplets ran down her cheeks like tears.

ONE

TRICK-OR-TREAT SUPPLIES

4 battle-magic pouches
1 portal pouch
1 thermos of pumpkin-spice tea
1 apple muffin
Sturdy boots
Unparalleled courage

Raven's Murk Castle, Wilds of Canada

Y*ou,*" Poppy Dyer muttered as a demon approached her, framed in the glow of lightning bolts.

Rök Kours, her nemesis. The mercenary she mused about far too often.

What was he doing at this castle? And how could she get rid of him before the moon rose?

He narrowed his smoky-blue eyes, their color vivid against his tanned skin. *"You."*

When he climbed the castle's steps to join her at the entry, she held her ground, yet her gaze couldn't help but sweep over his chiseled features with appreciation—his wide jaw, strong chin, and aquiline nose.

She got lost for a moment when she met those heavy-lidded eyes before she dragged her focus upward. His thick black hair was long enough to tie back in a queue, but tonight he wore it loose to cover most of his silvery horns. Over the years she'd seen them flared with aggression—and once with passion.

His demon-may-care attitude matched his appearance. A frayed, navy T-shirt highlighted his muscular chest and arms, and his worn jeans clung to his narrow hips. Scuffed boots and a sword belted around his waist rounded out the ensemble.

He looked tired though, as if he'd just rolled out of bed from his latest conquest. Likely.

Finding her voice, she said, "I wish I could say this was a pleasure, but it never is with you." She was proud of how calm she sounded when unwelcome chemistry simmered between them like a bubbling potion.

It temporarily overrode her nerves about tonight's mission: breach this castle at moonrise, find her prize, then get out during the brief window at moonset.

"*Never* a pleasure?" Rök's rumble of a voice pricked her senses. "You know that's a lie." His lips curved into a slow, mind-scrambling smile that showed off white teeth with a hint of his demon fangs. "You liked my kiss well enough."

Their sole kiss on their sole date.

Two years ago, when he'd slanted his mouth over hers in the rain, she'd moaned with abandon and dug her nails into his back, her body desperate for his.

Her body was a fucking idiot. "Will you never stop bringing that up?" Would she never stop replaying the feel of those lips?

Rain-wetted, demon-hot.

His talented tongue was pointed—

"As soon as you stop staring at my mouth like you fancy another one."

She darted her gaze away. "I don't have time for your games tonight. Some of us are on the clock." And much was on the line.

She glanced past him to survey the two-hundred-room castle. Lightning flashed behind its gravity-defying towers. Thunder clapped: *BOOM BOOM.* A nearby pond gave up sulfurous fumes. Dead spruces circled it, limned in silver flickers.

To complete the property's ill-omened look, a cemetery lined one side of the overgrown drive. The tombstones were all askew, like a witch's hat after a bender. A couple of ghouls skulked amidst the weathered stones.

This castle was the most foreboding place she'd ever beheld, and that was something for a witch to say. The wizard who'd built it had been a Lore philanthropist and a gifted scientist, until his family had died under mysterious circumstances a century ago.

No one had ever spied him outside these walls again, but her coven hadn't sensed his death until a few decades later. So what had he been up to in the intervening years? Some whispered that he'd gone rogue, turning balls-out evil.

BOOM.

She felt the thunder in her stomach, along with clenching nerves. Steeling herself, she adjusted her cross-body satchel with her few spell pouches inside. She'd had scant time to prepare for tonight and hadn't been able to ask her sisters for help.

They'd never suspected she would set off by herself for this particular mission, but by now, they would know she'd given them the slip.

One of the last mistakes I'll ever make?

Drawing her from that unsettling thought, Rök said, "You

assume I'm not on the clock as well?" After letting his gaze roam over her from her boots to her bright-red hair, he leaned against the entry wall and crossed his brawny arms over his chest. A lesser witch would have gawked. His sculpted seven-foot-tall body was as seductive as the most gripping enchantment. "Who hired you to come here?"

"Spill info on my client?" When she gave him an indulgent smile, his attention clocked her curving lips, making her cheeks heat. "What kind of merc would I be?" In truth, no one had hired her. She was here to risk her life, on this, the most problematic of nights, to break a curse.

So who had hired Rök? Did his presence mean other mercs would show?

"You up for pooling intel on this place?" His accent was British-adjacent, peppered with American slang. When they'd talked for hours on their date, she'd learned he'd been raised in Rothkalina, the rage demon kingdom, but his parents had bounced around until Rök's first Accession when they'd both died in battle.

"Not a chance. I know everything I need to know." Her research indicated that a pressurized boundary spell surrounded the structure. When the veil between worlds was thinnest—during a full moon on Halloween night—the castle door would swing open once the moon rose.

Getting out would prove more precarious. After all, none of the explorers had returned from the last expedition into the interior. . . .

The Halloween timing was unfortunate since her own curse burgeoned out of control on this night. Any moment now, the monsters she unwillingly created once a year would wake.

The idea of this demon seeing them made her cheeks heat again. "In fact, you should leave and spare yourself a defeat. Tell me, Rök, what will it take to get you gone?" His lids went heavy as they always did whenever she said his name. *Such a player, such an act.* Had she once fallen for his charm? *Almost.* "Half of my bounty?" *My nonexistent bounty.*

"We're in a may-the-best-demon-win situation here, and I intend to claim everything that's coming to me," he said, a hint of warning in his tone.

"I've always held my own with you whenever the two of us have faced off. I can handle whatever you bring into the mix."

Her words seemed to please him. "True. You give as good as you get."

Why did she feel as if he was speaking about something else entirely? "What's going on here? You're being weird."

He shrugged. "Strange day."

Rain began to fall. He glanced out over the grounds, then back at her, his irises changing color—often a sign of high emotion in immortals. When his blue eyes turned gray like spotlit smoke, she almost convinced herself he was replaying their kiss. But a male like him, who went through so many paramours, probably didn't remember it.

Drops swelled into a deluge. Water poured along the edge of the nearby overhang, creating a lightning-lit curtain. On this covered portico, she and Rök might as well have been alone together in a cocoon. Their breaths sounded loud, their heartbeats syncing. . . .

Poppy barely noticed when the wind picked up, dispersing the heavy downpour. She and the demon stood staring at each other, wordless, until a lightning bolt detonated nearby.

Inner shake. "Strange day, demon? Then you should go home now and enjoy the draw."

He blinked, as if he'd lost the thread of their conversation. "Maybe I came here hoping to see you."

"Uh-huh. I wish I could lie as easily as demons seem to," she said, though she'd never sensed him lying to her, not once in all their interactions.

"Can you not tell I'm attracted to you?"

Yes, but . . . "You're more attracted to the chase. I'm the only single female you haven't been able to seduce, which makes me an anomaly in the Lore: the lay that got away."

"*Hmm.*" That sound rumbled from his broad chest, telling her nothing, sending her thoughts tripping about like a horror-movie damsel. He levered himself away from the wall and strode over beside her.

Sensation crackled along her skin from his mere nearness. His heady scent was a mix of mist and embers.

"So how do we handle tonight?"

Collecting herself, she said, "You can surrender now and salvage some of your pride. My streak is only going to continue." That wasn't true. The last time the two of them had gone head-to-head, she'd been hired to protect a warlord's daughter from an unfitting suitor. That suitor had hired Rök to steal the female away.

One problem: the beautiful daughter had wanted to be stolen *by Rök*, had sneaked out from Poppy's protection, straight into the demon's arms.

Left fuming over her lost pay, Poppy had thought the two would hole up in some lair and make like rabbits. Instead, Rök had dropped off the woman with friends before returning to Poppy. All nonchalant, he'd asked, "You like fancy restaurants?" She'd agreed to a date partly out of sheer curiosity.

"Surrender?" he scoffed now. "Oh, Red, I've won against you as much as I've lost."

"Oh, player, I've nothing to worry about. You'll get summoned before we enter the castle, and the night will be mine." Any woman who slept with a smoke demon could summon him at will. Over the centuries, he'd racked up an army of these swimbos—a play on She Who Must Be Obeyed—so he was prone to vanish.

During Poppy's date with him, he'd been summoned by a lover and had never returned. Which was for the best.

He grinned. "Is there anything sexier than a jealous witch? If there is, I can't think of it."

"I am not jealous." *Hand up if you're a jealous witch. Me, me!* "Look, if you leave now, I'll walk on the next job."

"Where's the sport in that? Besides, I could just teleport you home and return here, snagging the prize for myself."

Her hand darted inside her bag to snare one of her magic pouches. "Try it, demon. Oh, *do.*"

He held up his palms in surrender. "Why would I beg off when I can see how much you want this gig?"

"Why do *you* want it so bad?" Poppy and the demon must be after the same thing. When she'd been told the answer to her curse lay within these walls, she'd pictured a magical talisman, a cursebreaker, that would set her free.

Rök's cagey look perked up her witchly acquisitiveness.

Tapping her chin, she said, "Are you in need of funds? Poor demon hasn't been saving his coin?" The most hazardous merc jobs were the most lucrative, and she'd heard that he'd signed on for one lethal mission after another, almost as if he had a death wish—or a huge debt. "Taking all your girlfriends to eat at pricey restaurants must empty your pockets."

"Hmm. Do I do that? In any case, I like to work. Keeps me young." He looked no more than thirty, but he was thirteen centuries old. "Admit it: mercs have fun . . ." He trailed off, his gaze flicking in the direction of the glowing ghouls.

Despite the earlier rain, their number had grown to three, a larger one and two smaller ones. Rök rested a hand on his sword.

Poppy didn't spook easily, but something about that trio filled her with disquiet. Keeping her tone light, she said, "Scared of a few ghouls?"

"Anybody with sense avoids them."

A scratch or bite could turn even an immortal into the undead. "Then off you go."

"Sticking around, if it's all the same."

Wasn't all the same; never would be after he'd hurt her so badly.

Rök gestured to the front door. "What are you waiting for?"

The boundary spell, duh. "You don't know?" His commitment to research usually rivaled hers.

"Checking to see if you do." His lazy grin made her more suspicious.

"Whatever." Spears of moonlight penetrated the clouds. It was time. Which meant she had no shot at losing him before the castle opened. Her muscles tensed with readiness, and she felt his attention like a touch.

A wave of mystical energy swelled from the building, swarming outward over them. The magic was dark, tasted bitter. *Am I ready to take on this castle?* She stared at the door. *Will I ever exit again?*

Maybe she should wait and prep more. Though everyone in her coven figured she was a conjurer (she had the most luck with those spell pouches), she'd demonstrated no innate caste power. And tonight, she had nothing except a handful of pouches and an activated curse.

Ergo: saddle up!

So foolish. Yet the next opportunity to enter—during another Halloween full moon—wouldn't be for nineteen years. Her curse would drive her insane by then.

When the door swung open with a hiss, she straightened her shoulders and started forward. *Here goes everything. . . .*

Rök muttered, "In over your head."

"Only way to swim." Inside she blinked against the gloom—she had no demonic night vision—until olden gas lights flickered on. Their dust-coated sconces painted the foyer in a harsh light.

"No one lives here, right?" Rök followed her in. "So who's paying the gas bill?"

"Powered by residual magic." Just like the boundary.

For such a sizable area, the air was stale. Cobwebs crisscrossed the floor and walls, but they looked old.

When Rök shadowed her steps, Poppy's heart thumped. She didn't want to spend a night trapped here with him, but she couldn't prevent him from staying unless she was ready to sacrifice a pouch.

She'd just have to lose him inside. Poppy was mystically sensitive; he wasn't. She would uncover the prize well before he could.

"Anybody home?" she called out into the echoing expanse. "Hellooo? Is anyone—"

The door slammed shut behind them. She and Rök whirled around. The hissing sound of pressurization proved more ominous than the castle's appearance.

Poppy had a feeling that this place promised hell, and she'd come to collect.

TWO

Chills skittered up Rök's back. He inhaled the air; remnants of blood and death greeted him.

Poppy was a formidable mercenary like him, but he suspected they were *both* in over their heads. Better to teleport her to safety and convince her to pick up where they'd left off two years ago. He grasped her arm. "We're leaving." Before she could protest, he teleported her.

Then blinked in confusion. They hadn't budged.

He tried again. Nothing.

"You asshole!" She yanked free of his hold. "You were going to trace me away? Oh, it's on."

He concentrated on teleporting across the dusty foyer. Failed. He tried to turn into smoke. Only a useless haze arose over his skin. He was a godsdamned smoke demon; he'd been able to fade into smoke since before his pup horns had first molted.

As the witch gazed on, he hastened to the front door. Couldn't open it. He kicked the wood and clawed at the frame, leaving not a scratch. He strode to the nearest window and launched his boot into the glass; got thrown backward. "What is this?"

"The boundary spell works from the inside too." Her amused tone rankled. "It won't open until tomorrow morning."

Disbelief. "We're trapped." Teleporting demons didn't do *trapped*. "Why can't I trace within these walls or turn to smoke?"

"Dunno. I don't sense any problem with my pouches. Must be a species-specific power dampener. Maybe the castle's owner hated smoke demons?"

"What owner?"

"A long-dead wizard. You really did zero research?"

He waved that away, checking his cell phone. "No bars? This is a Wiccan LoreLine!" Despite his distance from civilization, he should still get reception. He shoved it back into his pocket. "What about yours?"

"Didn't bring one. Even if I need help, no one can breach the entry."

"You're cool with that?"

"What can I say? I dig cheap thrills."

Her words distracted him. *Ah, witch, I can provide the cheapest, filthiest thrills you ever imagined. . . .*

No! Head in the game, Rök. "Use one of your spells for a portal out of here." She always had one handy for her work.

Scoffing laugh. "I'm not tapping out because my adversary has cold feet."

"I'm not your adversary." He ran a hand over his nape. "Everything about this castle is *wrong*. I know your senses are like a rock's, but you have to feel how off this place is."

She tapped her chin with a pink nail, so unlike his black claws. "A wizard's bespelled fortress? From which the previous expedition failed to surface? With some ghouls for curb appeal? Nah, feels great."

He ignored her sarcasm. "They didn't surface?"

Her grin was cheery. "Not one explorer."

"How much would it take for you to abandon this mission?"

She read his obvious unease and gave another laugh. "What's the matter? Never had a mission hiccup?" She turned to check the coat closet—empty—then investigated the statuettes along the perimeter of the foyer. "Even if I wanted to open a portal, which I don't, it would just transport me to another part of the castle."

"Then how do we get out of here?"

She must've taken pity on him because she answered, "According to legend, the door will reopen for a short interval when the moon sets."

The setting of a full moon corresponded to sunrise. Had he ever been so ready for dawn? "How short of an interval?"

"A raven will call four times from a spruce by the pond."

"Four calls. Of a raven." Rök had heard of sketchier shit in the Lore. At the same time, not much was random in the world of immortals. *Random* usually meant he hadn't discovered the pattern yet. So why did this castle open under such precise circumstances? "And if we miss the grand opening?"

"We'll be stuck here until the next Halloween full moon."

His jaw slackened. "That only happens every twenty years or so."

"Yup."

Magic might power the lights, but that didn't mean they'd find decades' worth of food and water inside. Generally only fire or a beheading could kill an immortal, but some Loreans perished from less. Could a witch of only a hundred years starve? "Tell me about the wizard. Why did he build this place?" What would Rök and Poppy face tonight?

"It was supposed to be a home for his family, but they died

a century ago." She peeked under a dust cover concealing a settee. What was she searching for? "The wizard sealed himself up inside until he kicked it a few decades back. Some say he lost his mind and was up to no good, while others say this castle is his booby-trapped tomb."

"Why would you come here without backup? Your sisters wouldn't have sent you off alone." He knew this for a fact, had run into the oldest Dyer sister earlier. Lea. Fearsome creature, that one.

But then, the five sisters were all formidable in their own ways, rumored to each possess a different witchly caste power.

Lea's piece of advice for him still resonated. He would never forget it because he replayed it every day. . . .

Poppy shrugged. "You know I work jobs by myself."

"And I've always wondered why." Rök had recently undertaken a slew of solo missions himself, but he preferred the camaraderie of a partner or a crew.

"Did you know that each of my sisters is named after a plant?"

He did. Oleander or Lea, Sage, Clover, and Belladonna. Herbalists and concoctionesses, they utilized plants in hex pouches.

Funny, though, when he'd taken Poppy to dinner, she'd ordered steak, rare. "Yeah, so?"

"So, I grow best with my own spot in the sun."

How could she be so cavalier? No job was worth her life. "Now you might be about to die in a dark castle. Plants do that too."

She winked at him.

Frustrating witch! "At least *try* to use your portal. I'll make it worth your while—"

Without another word, she started across the foyer, heading deeper into the castle. Her boot heels clicked against stone, her jeans rasping between her shapely thighs.

He watched her sexy stride for heart-stopping seconds. At least she tempered some of his teleporter's claustrophobia. If he had to be trapped with anyone, he'd choose Poppy.

What a fitting name.

Pretty flower. Ruinous drug.

When he'd first encountered her on jobs, he hadn't considered her anything special to look at with her bright hair scraped back in a bun and her serviceable work clothes. She had nice features and eyes the color of a new leaf, but nothing to make him do a double take.

Her scent though. It'd gotten him as randy as a stag encountering its first dose of heat.

In concoction terms, her scent was three parts vitality and one part smoky poppy blossoms, with a hint of womanly arousal. In other words: smoke-demon nirvana. So of course Rök had asked her out.

When she'd let down her hair for their date and he'd seen all those glorious locks framing her heart-shaped face, he'd been enraptured.

The little middle gap in her white teeth? Adorable. The glimmer in those green eyes as she'd mocked his best seduction lines? Made him hard. The sight of her curves in a rain-dampened dress? *Gods below have mercy on this demon.*

Yet after one tiny hiccup, she'd ditched their date. When she'd finally agreed to another one, the capricious witch had stood him up and blocked his number!

She was attracted to him—who wasn't?—but it hadn't been enough to bring her back for more. In fact, she'd avoided him for two years, dating someone else for half of that time.

He watched her for a moment more—*mercy on this demon*—then traced to catch up.

And didn't go anywhere. That was going to take some

getting used to. "Heading right into danger?" he asked as he jogged to her side. "Your pay must be astronomical."

She strode toward a grand staircase, leaving a wake of disturbed cobwebs. "I'm very motivated. Your client paying you well?"

He'd let her believe he had a client; he did not have a client. "Would I ever take a job with measly pay?" Not a lie.

"Yet a spymaster like you didn't research?" She shook her head, and a long curl escaped her bun, the color stark against her leather jacket.

"Didn't get a chance to." His former merc partner, Cadeon the Kingmaker, would razz Rök about the amount of research he usually did. Tonight's preparation? Several demon brews and a blind leap into the unknown. "You could say this was a last-minute opportunity. I heard something tasty was here and wanted to jump all over it."

Looking titillated, she said, "Spill."

"As soon as you do," he countered, wondering how to explain his actions. *Well, I was at Erol's bar, roiling inside, contemplating how selfish a prick I might be—*

Skittering sounded from the floors above, drawing his attention. "What's the intel on the castle's bogeys? Could be kobolds up there." Those gnome monsters worked in packs to take down unsuspecting Loreans.

"I'm sure it's just rats."

His horns all but twitched. *She's lying.* Over the years, he'd discovered that she was a piss-poor dissembler. But why lie? He sensed impending danger.

Good. He welcomed it, felt more firmly in his comfort zone. Yet she looked uneasy. "Never had a mission hiccup, Red?"

Straightening her shoulders, she plowed on. "You should go your way, and I'll go mine."

Why'd she find it so bloody easy to *not* be around him?

Females the worlds over clamored for his attention—he could get summoned ten times a night—but not Poppy Dyer. "We might as well work together. If we teamed up, I could take the clout and give you the prize."

"How about I take the clout and the prize and give *you* a swift kick to the balls?"

Her attitude made his head buzz like a potent aphrodisiac. "I've missed your humor, witch."

They'd just reached the stairs when the skittering intensified, like a rave club full of kobolds. She swerved from the steps and headed toward another hallway.

He followed. "You're not curious what's up there?"

She shook her head, her bun loosening more.

What he wouldn't give to release that silky mane and thread his fingers through it. "Where are you going?"

"I think the basement is this way. I plan to explore this castle from bottom to top." He'd just parted his lips to make a quip when she pointed at him over her shoulder and said, "Don't."

The skittering suddenly sounded as if it was coming from the floor *below* them.

"On second thought . . ." She backtracked to another hallway. "I'll start my investigation here."

"You're avoiding trouble! You've never been timid before." The witch was often the first into the fray. "Maybe your bag of tricks isn't as full as it should be." On past gigs, she'd come equipped with that satchel full of pouches. Had she gone off half-cocked tonight?

"As usual, I'm completely prepared." She patted her bag with her customary confidence. Still, he sensed she was lying. "I'm just following my gut. Feel free to get lost. I'll meet you at the front entrance in"—she checked her sports watch—"eight hours. I'll be the one holding the prize." With that, she headed through a pair of double doors.

Get lost, she'd said. Gods below, he'd tried.

He pictured his secluded cabin in Iceland. How many nights had he traced/paced in front of the fire? Enough to wear two holes into the floor! More holes dotted the wooden walls from when he'd rammed his aching horns with frustration.

Always on his mind was the question: *Am I a decent male?*

He'd booked treacherous jobs, but there were only so many. Though Cade and his mate Holly welcomed him to their home, Rök didn't want to intrude too much. Eventually his inner turmoil would drive him to Erol's, yet even in a crowd of Loreans, Rök felt isolated.

With a muttered curse, he followed Poppy through the doors into an expansive kitchen sparsely lit with more gas lamps. A crew of cooks must've once prepared meals here for scores of Loreans.

Poppy's covetous gaze swept the area, as if she could see past the cobwebs dangling from pot racks and the chalky rat droppings on the countertops.

"I'll never understand the inner workings of the Wiccan mind. You're looking at this kitchen as though you're ready to move in."

Shrug. "I like them big." He'd just opened his mouth for a joke when she warned, *"Don't."*

He refrained from knocking her softball pitch into the innuendo bleachers. "Fair enough. Why do you like big kitchens?"

As if the words were pulled from her, she said, "My sisters and I live in an old Victorian manor." *I know. Been there.* "And our kitchen isn't huge. We don't have enough room for concocting *and* making meals. Something had to give, so we don't cook as much as we'd like."

"I thought all of you Louisiana witches wanted to live amid your coven." Andoain, the newly inaugurated seat of the House of Witches in this realm, was located outside New Orleans.

"The Andoain witches are a bit . . ."

"Overserved?" The coven was like a party-hearty sorority house from a slasher flick. Except these sorority girls would slash back. With magic.

"I was going to say *young*, but your observation is fair. When my parents left the realm for a stint, my sisters and I voted to stay at their place."

Her folks were the rare witch/warlock superpower couple living in perfect mystical symbiosis or whatever. He'd heard they were hard-core practitioners, teachers of the occult. After their daughters had all reached immortality, the couple had returned to the Wiccae dimension of Akelarre to hone their deep witchery for the coming Accession.

This one was shaping up differently from past Accessions. Instead of unrelenting skirmishes, Loreans feared a great war between an alliance of factions in this realm and the enigmatic Møriør. . . .

When Poppy checked some of the cupboards, Rök said, "I don't scent a crumb of food here." A few decomposed rats dotted the tiled floor, confirming that no food existed—and that the sealed castle prevented even a rodent's escape. "I don't suppose you've got a never-ending energy bar in that bag of yours?"

"Nope. One thermos of tea and a muffin."

"Well, that'll certainly keep us till the next Halloween full moon."

She blinked up at him. "Us?"

Skittering sounded from the corners of the kitchen. "We're

not alone." He freed his sword and scented the air, detecting something unexpected: scales.

Red eyes appeared in the shadows, what must be a legion of small, befanged creatures with scaly green skin. "Are those . . ." He frowned, recalling where he'd seen such creatures before. ". . . gremlins?" He turned to Poppy and read her expression: zero surprise. "You knew they'd be here?"

"Just ignore them." She headed toward the kitchen doors. A dozen more of them blocked her way.

"Stay behind me." Sword raised, he hastened in front of her, cursing his inability to trace her away. "How is this possible? They don't exist in the Lore." They didn't exist at all, except in the minds of humans.

"I said to ignore them." She sidled around to face him. "They can't hurt you. They're just illusions."

Her irises had turned purple like sunstruck lavender. "Your eyes are alight." His narrowed. A witch's eyes could glow from emotion, but also from power. "Are *you* making these?"

"It's involuntary, okay?"

Her ability reminded him of Sabine, the Sorceri Queen of Illusions. Sabine was considered the queen because she could conjure sights and sounds better than anyone else alive. But others could also dabble with the same talent. "How do you know these are just illusions?" The gremlins climbed the countertops, positioning themselves to strike. "I can scent them."

Poppy marched up to the mass of slavering creatures. "Look." She reached toward a larger one. "It can't hurt me."

The thing gave a snarl, baring its mouth full of fangs. Then it leapt for her face.

THREE

Poppy had trained herself not to react. "It's just an illu—"
Rök vaulted in front of her, wielding his long sword. *Slash.*
He severed a *very real gremlin* in two!

No time for shock; the remaining creatures attacked, springing off the countertops.

Rök cut through a swath of them. "Illusion, huh? They wet my blade readily enough." Green blood coated it.

She snagged a pouch from her bag. It disintegrated into her palm as battle magic churned through her—like a hit of Hecate's divinity. Purple light shone from her hands. When more gremlins leapt for her, she released beams from her palms. The creatures burst, reptilian body parts painting the walls. "This has never happened!"

"What the hell is going on here?" Rök sent fang-filled heads tumbling.

She picked off any that got past the reach of his blade. "I think someone cursed me, turning any conjuring potential I might have against me, forcing me to fuel the illusions. Maybe it was a rogue warlock. Or a rival merc hired a traitorous witch. If we'd met sooner, I might have suspected you!"

He scowled. "When did it start?" *Slash* went his sword.

Blast went her beams. "Decades ago. I'd spot something amiss out of the corner of my eye, but only on Halloween night." As he defended to his left, more attacked on his right. She exploded them to the ceiling. "I thought I was imagining it. Then they got worse each year. But they've never embodied before!"

"Then what gives?"

As she fought beside Rök, she played out different explanations, settling on the most likely: "Maybe this place is intensifying the curse." A wizard's stronghold imbued with magic? She could see it.

If the castle wouldn't open until dawn and it was turning her illusions into physical manifestations, then she was in trouble. She had every reason to expect many more, and they would only get deadlier.

"Kind of random, no?" Rök moved with the ease of a practiced warrior, all his generous muscles working together to slaughter his enemy. "Gremlins?"

A pair vaulted from a pot rack, heading for a dismount— on her head. She blasted them into oblivion, then admitted, "Not just gremlins."

"What else?" He skewered three like a scaly kabob.

She reluctantly said, "Anything that haunts mortals on Halloween. Horror villains and monsters." She knew Rök was well versed in them. "They change over time. I call them my *visitors*." Whenever human nightmares updated, so too would the visitors. "Over the last few years, I've seen a doll with a knife. A killer clown. Sometimes aliens and . . ." She hesitated, not wanting to cop to the most problematic one.

Rök flung the gremlin kabob from his blade. *"And?"*

"The . . . Headless Horseman. Or, at least, the humans' latest version of it." The last time she'd encountered the methodical swordsman and his red-eyed steed, she'd thanked Hecate he wasn't real. Would he be tonight?

"You mean the version that hunts heads and can't be killed? Fantastic."

"I can't control this! You think I haven't tried to? They've haunted me!" She would wake to a maniac with a glove of razors looming over her bed. The machete-wielding camp slasher had first greeted her in the bathroom—the last shower she'd ever take after sunset on Halloween.

Dreading the coming visitation, she'd sought help from Mariketa, the leader of the House of Witches. Just a week ago, the young witch had told her that she'd find the answer to her curse within this castle. Poppy had believed the curse would be broken here—not enhanced!

"What do they want?" Rök's sword never slowed.

"They've terrorized anyone who's seen them." Like her poor sisters. Poppy hadn't told her parents how bad it'd gotten, refusing to distract them from their training. "Now that the visitors are embodied, I think senseless killing is the name of the game for them."

"Kill you? You're fueling them. Where's the logic in that?"

"Gremlins: masters of logic." She blew a lock of hair out of her eyes and fired again. "You want me to call a time-out and ask them about their motivations?"

"You're certain this is a curse? Maybe it's your own power gone berserk."

"A witch's power rarely harms her, and she gathers more control over time, not less. But even so, I wasn't fully convinced it was a curse until now."

"Why now?"

Two gremlins clambered across the floor toward her legs, earning a blast. "Because they *are* trying to kill me."

"Then why take a job at bloody Halloween?"

"The castle would only open tonight!"

Rök muttered, "Wiccans, man," as he beheaded another pair.

She fired on a slavering trio, exploding them like meat sauce in a microwave. The demon cast her a brief look of approval. Only four left, but her borrowed magic was fading.

With an expert sweep of his sword, Rök struck the four down. A row of heads flew, landing with thuds to roll across the floor.

His chest heaved as they scanned the twitching bodies. "Should we be expecting more of these fuckers?"

"I don't think so."

He lowered his gore-covered sword.

"But other visitors will appear," she added.

Bitter laugh. "Course they will."

The light across her palms sputtered. Fueling her spells *and* the visitors always depleted her magic, which must be the point of the curse.

Rök met her gaze with his brows drawn. "Your eyes are back to normal for now."

Did she detect worry in his troubled expression? Not for himself but *for her*? As they stared at each other, emotions best left buried crept to the surface. She rubbed her neck, feeling as if she was on the precipice of something more perilous than even the visitors. . . .

Rök turned from her, ending the charged moment. He swiped his sword on a dusty dish towel and sheathed it. Since Poppy was the source of these killers, his safest bet would be to leave her behind and get on with his job.

True to form, he left her without a word. *There he goes, out of here at the first sign of trouble.*

She stared at the doors closing behind him. She'd wanted away from him, hadn't she? Forced proximity for an entire night would've been unbearable.

So why this dejection? She was on a mission, not another ill-fated date. What a farce that had been, stranded by him at the most expensive restaurant in the Lore.

Two years ago
New Orleans

"Ellen Ripley in the furnace," Poppy told Rök as they enjoyed scrumptious wine imported from Sylvan, oysters from Sargasoe, and a debate about the best character sacrifices in horror flicks.

In other words, the perfect date.

"Ripley? Agree to disagree, Red." He grinned over his wineglass, emanating sex appeal. He looked so decadent in his bespoke suit that he should come with a health warning. "I think the best sacrifices arise when there's still a bit of hope that the character can be saved. Once the alien implanted in Ripley, all hope was lost. She just took that plot development to its logical conclusion in the coolest way."

He knew his *Alien* lore! As the proud co-owner of a black cat named Newt, Poppy was impressed. High from Rök's undivided attention, she leaned forward in her chair, chin propped on her hand, hearts in her eyes. Fellow diners kept staring at them, must sense the chemistry sparking between Rök and her.

For the umpteenth time tonight, she mused, *What if I am*

his mate? He might not even realize it. Or was he feeling the same connection?

They'd shared similar interests, swapping merc tips and movie trivia. He'd laughed at her jokes and genuinely seemed to like her. And the attraction . . . Well, they hadn't even made it to the front steps of the restaurant before they'd assailed each other. A selfie in the parking lot had turned into the best kiss of her life—and it'd only whetted her appetite for more of him.

When she was getting ready for the night earlier, her sisters had gathered in her room, warning her against going out with one of the Lore's most notorious players. Lea had said, "You told us you wanted to settle down, right? You know you're destined for a warlock. A demon can't protect you from magic, but a warlock could. A fellow Wiccan could even help you defeat your curse."

This was . . . a good point. Their parents were an example of how witches and warlocks could amplify each other's abilities. In any Wiccan calculation, more magic was always better than less magic. "It's just a casual date," Poppy had assured everyone.

After the four sisters had taken bets that one of Rök's lovers would hail him before the dinner concluded, Sage had summed up their thoughts: "Demons are like bulls: horned and raring to chase any old red cape."

Ha! How wrong they'd been. *I'm not any old red cape.*

And this was not just a casual date; something was happening here.

Keeping up with the conversation, Poppy pointed out, "Bishop II's offer to remove the alien from Ripley could have been real. Though I don't think her character would ever accept that the alien inside her might live."

"Exactly." The gleam in Rök's eyes made her feel praised. "Just like the priest who dove out of the window in *The Exorcist.*

He couldn't live with the idea that the demon might survive, which, by the way, stung a little."

She chuckled at his aggrieved look. "So, what's your best character sacrifice?"

He thought for a moment. "The dad in *A Quiet Place*. His chances before his death were better than nil, but he would do anything to save his beloved children."

"You would've yelled and drawn the monster away from them?"

Rök held her gaze. "When you love something, you protect it."

She swallowed, so caught up in this demon she could drown in him.

Caution warned, *Just dip a toe.*

Experience screamed, *Do not head in deeper.*

Desire whispered, *Headfirst and make a splash.*

Rök reached across the table and took her hand, leaning in to press his lips to the pulse point at her wrist.

"Player," she murmured. "You've got your moves down, don't you?"

He grinned against her skin. "And you keep calling me out on them. . . ." He trailed off, his body beginning to *blur.* "Poppy—"

Her name seemed to echo for a beat as he vanished, leaving her hand in midair and the chair across from her empty.

She straightened, collecting herself. He would return directly; he just needed to tell the summoner that he was on a date. Rök had warned her that he sometimes disappeared.

Still, she wondered what he'd find when he answered that call. A naked temptress already in the throes? Would a player resist?

Pouring herself more pricey wine, Poppy waited for him.

She waited.

She waited.

Her imagination went wild. She quaffed another glass and fielded commiserating looks from other female patrons.

After an hour passed, Poppy finally accepted that Rök was off screwing someone else while their entrees grew chilled and her wine bottle drained.

Had she actually thought something special was occurring between her and the demon? Her public humiliation in this upscale place didn't touch her private humiliation. Her sisters had been right. For males like Rök, one woman was as good as another.

The eye-watering bill added salt to the wound. As Poppy dazedly meandered out of the restaurant and through that memorable parking lot, she felt a mix of grief and fury. *Grury.* Rök made her *grurious.*

She'd foolishly believed that he was the one for her.

The one.

Unfortunately, he considered her something else.

One of many.

FOUR

Rök glanced over his shoulder, expecting to see a grateful witch following on his heels. "Poppy?" Out of habit, he tried to trace back to her, failed, then barged through the kitchen doors.

Surrounded by gremlin carnage, she narrowed her gaze at him.

"The hell, Red? This is where we leave. You said there's going to be more." Despite all his research—he'd gathered intel on her as if she were a mission—he'd uncovered no hint of this curse. His thoughts bounced to the night of their date; certain puzzle pieces were falling into place. "We need to get to a better battleground. So I say this in all seriousness: *Come with me if you want to live.*" He offered his hand.

The witch didn't take it, but she did exit the reeking kitchen with him.

In the hallway, she stopped. "What's your angle, demon?"

"What are you talking about?" His angle? *Keeping this stubborn female alive.* She was right; she *was* an anomaly in the Lore. The two of them had unfinished business to take care of.

"The visitors will stick close to me, so all you have to do is steer clear. Complete your job and minimize risks—those two things are pretty much all a merc focuses on."

"I'm not going to abandon you."

"No, you would *never* do that," she said in a sarcastic tone. "Oh, come on, Rök. We're enemies."

"Poppy, *no*." How had they gotten so sideways on this? Because he'd been summoned during their date? He was a smoke demon; swimbos bloody happened.

"Do you know how many times I've almost collected the reward on your head?"

Rök had a few bounties on him, and maybe some orders to "terminate with extreme prejudice." People thought two dimensions had issued them. Nonsense. *Fifteen*. He had a way of making dimensional warlords very unhappy—just because females preferred Rök. "For a bag of coin, you would turn me in to be executed?"

"Not at all," she said grandly. "More for bragging rights."

So godsdamned sideways. "Doesn't matter. I've decided I'm going to protect you tonight."

"What job would you ditch without a care?"

He wasn't ready to explain everything, but he would never lie to her, so he fell back on one of his strengths: flirtation. "That battle back there, beauty? Was our *foreplay*. Screw any job I might have had. I'm only interested in picking up where we left off two years ago." If they could get away from this place, he could up his game and seduce her at last. *The lay that got away?* Not for much longer. "The wizard must've left behind a mystical power source. Let's find this castle's battery, shut it down, and teleport out of here early."

She crossed her arms over her chest. The movement made her jacket lapels gape and pulled her V-neck tight over her breasts.

Don't stare, don't stare. . . . But had he ever seen such mouthwatering breasts? *Head in the game, Rök.* With danger about, he didn't need to be fantasizing about this witch's pert—

"Even if I wanted to leave with you, which I don't, I'm not going anywhere till my job is complete."

He yanked his head up in disbelief. "We're starring in our very own horror movie! And how do characters get into trouble? When they won't leave the scene."

Her green eyes glinted with determination. "Some of us are professionals who don't spook lightly."

"I'm a demon of many years. I'm not the one in jeopardy here." Immortals grew stronger with age.

She raised her chin a notch—her way of unwillingly conceding a point. Yet she didn't budge. "You had your chance with me. Move on. I did."

After she'd stood him up on what should have been their second date, he'd gone to Rothkalina to bury himself in work. By the time he returned to this plane, she'd taken up with a warlock, some asshole named Ixius the Bringer. Ah, but the two of them had broken up a couple of weeks ago. "Why would I move on? I like a challenge. You're just waving a red cape in front of a bull."

Her coral-shaded lips parted as if he'd said something outrageous. "That's the thing about bulls. They're not very discerning." She turned from him and started down another hallway.

Sconces cast a gloomy light over the threadbare carpet and paneled walls as he caught up with her.

When she glared, he said, "Take the assist. You needed it back there."

Prickling with irritation, she strode on, her gaze keen for bogeys.

He figured her visitors would be the biggest danger, so

he'd monitor her eyes. When he and the witch passed a section of floral wallpaper, he said, "Nice decor. The atmosphere reminds me of the Overlook Hotel, only with a touch more REDRUM."

He could joke now—he was high on her and chuffed to have protected her—but earlier today? He'd been between jobs, his emotions roiling as usual; trace/pacing and horn abuse all around.

She barely spared him a glance. "So you like horror movies."

"Which you well remember. A love of the genre is just one of the many things we have in common." He frowned. "You do remember, right?"

"I'm surprised you do. How do you keep all your females straight?"

Don't. Ignoring her question, he said, "Cade and I made a pastime of drinking brew and binge-watching horror movies to see how much the humans got right about the Lore. At least, we used to, before his Valkyrie mate came along."

Lured into conversation, Poppy said, "I know Holly well."

"I figured." Witches and Valkyries were thick as thieves. Rök had suspected anything he told Cade might be passed on to Holly and from her to Poppy, so he'd kept his own counsel with his best friend.

"I talk to her often." Poppy's gaze flitted to Rök's horns. Had Holly told her how demons loved to have them stroked?

Rök's mouth went dry when Poppy fisted her satchel's strap in both hands. The idea of her silken palms handling him like that . . .

She cleared her throat. "Holly and Cadeon are a good couple. Unexpected, but good."

Rök dragged his gaze from her hands. "They're happy together. Weren't really before. Are now." He took in Poppy's stunning profile as he said, "One plus one equals two, huh?"

"And two more."

"Yeah, twin girls." They'd had them not long ago. Cade, the ruthless mercenary, had turned into a devoted mate and father. Love and laughter filled his and Holly's home with the toddlers. "Those are the cutest halflings you ever saw." Rök couldn't stop a grin. "They chase me everywhere, tracing after me. Uncle Rök is putty. I spend way too much time shopping for Duplos and dinosaurs."

She raised an auburn brow. "The big, bad merc has a soft spot for kids?"

"Didn't figure me for it either." But when Brianna and Alyson had first babbled happily to see him . . . ?

Putty.

"I thought you would retire when Cadeon did," Poppy said. "You must miss his guidance on jobs."

Rök's fond smile faded. "Guidance? I was the strategist for our team." After years of rivalry, he and Cade had joined forces. Their talents had been complementary. Rök lived for spy intrigues and intel; Cade lived to indiscriminately hack at foes with his sword.

Not that Rök didn't enjoy the feel of a blade slicing open a challenger, but the nimble gathering of intel . . . that was on a different level.

"Strategist, huh?" She tapped her chin. "You know, that explains a lot."

"We were the most successful crew in the Lore!"

"If you exclude the witches, I suppose."

"You heard about our Viper Terrace Offensive, right?"

She cast him a bored glance. "Mediocre."

"The Giant's Achilles Job?"

"Yawning."

"The Centaur Infiltration? Sneaking into the royal stable took more than a fake tail—"

"You were with a crew of demons each time," she pointed out. "Even against a giant, it's like punching down."

"I gathered intelligence against Omort the Deathless." The evil sorcerer who'd seized control of Rothkalina. "And our crew was there the night death finally caught up to that fucker." They'd defeated Omort's fire demon allies.

"Yet you didn't strike the blow."

Shade usually had no effect on Rök, but hers did. He excelled at his job and found it urgent for her to know that. He'd have to show her. "Working with others is the smartest play. Maybe you and I should team up more often." A couple of times in the past, he'd lent his fighting weight to help her out. He suspected she'd grudgingly aided him with a bit of magic too on occasion.

Or maybe that was just wishful thinking.

"I would never partner with someone who gets summoned so often."

He parted his lips to reply, but her criticism was fair. Cade had complained of the same. Though demon breeds could be summoned in various ways, smoke demons formed pacts with sex partners. To break the pact, Rök would have to publicly forsake the female, a cruel prospect. He figured they'd stop summoning him once he'd claimed his mate.

At the end of the hallway was a wooden door. The worn boards and rusted hinges screamed *basement*. Poppy headed right for it.

"So you're the character who traipses into the castle's dark basement?" In an ominous tone, he breathed, *"Don't go in there."*

She kind of grinned, reminding him of how he'd made her laugh on their date.

Then she seemed to harden herself against him. "I'm the witch who said she'd comb this place and is able to hold her own. If something lurks down there, maybe it should fear me. Maybe *I* am the scariest thing in this castle."

Sure thing. He applauded her confidence, but a more realistic view of her abilities would only help her. Without her usual stash of pouches, she'd be fighting with one hand tied behind her back.

Poppy Dyer hadn't achieved her full potential. Would she ever if he got his way?

She opened the door with a creaking groan so perfect someone should record it for a horror soundtrack. A few flickering wall sconces illuminated a steep stairway.

He inhaled the musty air. "This isn't a basement. It's a dungeon. The smell of the prisoners might as well be etched into the stone." He could still scent their desperation.

When Poppy started down, he gripped her shoulder. "Wait." A charge seemed to flow from her body to his until he had to bite back a groan.

She whirled around, giving his hand an arch look. "What?"

"Tell me what you're searching for." What could coax her down those steps?

"Why should I trust you with any more information? How about I tell you as soon as you divvy what brought you here?"

Not the time for *that* conversation. Instead of answering, he maneuvered around her. "If you're determined to go down there, at least follow me in."

A mercenary at heart, she waved him on.

The temperature grew colder as they descended to the dungeon. Inside, their steps echoed, indicating a large underground space. "You sensing anything magical? Maybe the castle's battery?"

"No." She peered around intently. "But . . . something."

He headed in deeper, finding several standard-issue cells, as well as a few openings that dotted the floor in a zigzag pattern. "Ah, oubliettes."

"Ooblee-what's?" Poppy asked from behind him.

"Oubliette means a place to forget. Prisoners were dumped into deep, cavernlike holes as a means of imprisonment—and execution."

"Wouldn't Lorean bodies still be down there, withered but clinging to life?"

Rök had a flashback of liberating starved immortals from Omort's personal dungeon. What he'd seen in those bloodstained cells would stay with him for eternity. "Unless they were too young to regenerate. But I don't scent anyone." Still stuck in that memory, he eased closer to the nearest oubliette. "How deep are these—"

"Wait!" she cried. "Those openings are bespelled."

He stepped back, giving his head a shake. "Thanks for the save."

"Had to do something. Since your mystical senses are like a rock's."

"Funny witch." He glanced around for something to toss in. He lobbed a loose brick near the opening, and some force sucked it down. *Whoosh.* He never heard it land. "Straight to hell, then."

"Even a demon like you might have trouble scaling up against that kind of pull."

He turned to her. "Let's get you away from them."

She frowned. "You've yet to give me a good reason you've turned . . . protective." She was suspicious; she should be.

"Though you might have no cause to trust me, I've never given you cause *not* to either. I've never lied to you, Poppy." One of Cade's rules for being a mercenary was to lie often, but he'd since learned his lesson. Rök too had learned.

"Maybe not. Yet you're hiding something from me. I don't know what, but *something*."

Oh, I am. Time for more distraction. "I do have an agenda." He moved closer to her, loving that she stood her ground. "I'll lend you my sword, and in exchange, I want another kiss." He'd do anything to repeat the one they'd shared, the most carnal kiss he'd ever experienced.

How many times had he stroked himself to the memory of it? He recalled her plush, breathless lips. Her nipples had been so stiff he'd felt them through his sport coat. When she'd pinned her knee to his hip to grind her sweet pussy against him, he'd nearly gone off. If someone hadn't honked and broken the moment, she might have received him right there.

Poppy scoffed. "You want me to kiss you? In your fantasies, demon."

"You star in them all, witch. Every night, I fantasize about stoking your lusts and sating you over and over." He lowered his voice seductively. "You always beg *more*. Until you beg *no more*. And I still make you come again."

Her breaths shallowed. She wasn't immune to him, so why avoid him? Maybe she only saw herself with a warlock.

Poppy recovered quickly enough. "Always back to sex with you. I'm not interested in a one-night stand, especially not an interrupted one. I'm looking for a romantic partner. You'll have to find someone else to be among your wild oats—I sowed my own seventy-five years ago when I froze into my immortality."

The idea of her *sowing* with other males . . . A rabid hellhound fed a strict diet of cocaine would feel more peaceable than Rök at that moment.

Then the rest of her words sank in. "Interrupted? You're stuck on this summoning point. I'd bet no one could summon me from this castle, so let's hit it right now."

She rolled her eyes. Were her irises glowing again?

He couldn't tell if they glowed from emotion or from the activation of her curse. "If you're not tempted, then why avoid me? Every time we've spied each other at Lore gatherings and neighborhood melees, you've portaled away."

"Get over yourself. Maybe I got bored seeing the same old faces."

"You said you want a romantic partner, yet you broke up with that warlock. Aren't warlocks prime dating material for witches?" Imagining those two together made Rök gnash his fangs.

"You heard about him?"

Rök was obsessed with intel and with Poppy. Of course he'd heard. "What happened?"

"Ixius wanted to take our relationship to the next level and asked me what I would bring to the table." Sliding Rök a take-no-bullshit smirk, she added, "So I told him I'd bring a hundred other warlocks who didn't ask stupid fucking questions."

That smirk drove him nuts. Rök growled with desire—

Rattle rattle rattle . . . sliiice.

He tensed at the new sound coming from outside the dungeon entrance. "Are those . . . rattling bones?" He unsheathed his sword and glanced at her eyes. Definitely aglow. "Let me guess: skeletons?"

"Wouldn't be Halloween without them. They're blocking the exit?"

"Naturally. But how bad can they be?"

Poppy's gaze took in their tricky position. "Historically, if you strike them, they'll reassemble. And they always come in number and armed with scythes."

"Fantastic." For more than a millennium, Rök had handled everything the Lore had thrown his way, as valiant as the night was long, but undead creatures creeped him out. Still . . . "I can defeat them," he told her, even though he was in close quarters with hungry oubliettes behind him.

His first instinct was to charge the stairs and bulldoze their way to more advantageous ground, but he had a vulnerable witch with him. "Stay behind me."

"Why?" She reached into her bag for another pouch.

"Because I'm a warrior with a sword. Spare your magic." Close-quarters battles weren't her strong suit anyway.

Amusement. "By all means. A male has the floor! Just don't do anything stupider than usual, demon."

"Great pep talk, Red."

Rattle rattle rattle . . . sliiice.

It was showtime. The visceral anticipation he felt before every battle hit him, the reminder that even his immortal life might be on the line.

He cast a glance at the witch. He'd be damned before hers was. Rök's ability to defend her from mystical shit like this had been called into question, but who was here now? Who was protecting her?

Me.

Just a couple of hours ago, he'd been downing mugs at Erol's. One word voiced in that noisy bar had turned him onto a completely different trajectory, one name.

Poppy.

FIVE

The demon readied for trouble, shoulders squared, his longsword reflecting the low light. His eyes were a brilliant gray, his fangs and horns sharpening. Smoke spun a hazy aura around his towering frame.

Magnificent male.

She might've expected the smoke to fill the room and choke her breaths, but it was more like shaded air. Over the years, she'd learned he could turn it thicker, using it for camouflage and even for travel.

Yet not in Raven's Murk Castle.

She struggled to stay focused on the incoming threat and to ignore her attraction to this demon. Why was he so protective after all this time? Why'd he have to talk about doting on kids with that devoted smile on his face?

Shake it off, Poppy. Rök Kours simply wasn't an option for her. She reminded herself of his reputation. He got off on the fact that paramours summoned him, like repeat customers who ranked him five stars.

Even if he weren't a player, he and Poppy still would have

no future. Though she'd once suspected she might be Rök's fated one, he had convinced her otherwise. Male Loreans went berserk if denied their mates.

Cadeon had held a siege for Holly; Rök hadn't even rung Poppy's freaking doorbell.

Somewhere out there, his female existed or would exist. Until he found that partner, Poppy would be a walk-on in the movie of his life.

And that was assuming he even wanted more than a one-night stand. That was assuming they lived through this night—

A pair of skeletons breached the dungeon's doorway, their bony feet clattering on the stone landing. Their menacing skulls craned left to right to scan the area.

Stray question: *How can they see? Or think?*

Stray answer: *They just fucking can.*

"That's messed up." Rök passed his sword from one hand to the other.

"You spooked yet?"

"Nothing in the Lore spooks me—except things that come back to life when they should be at their rest."

This unexpected admission only endeared him to her. He wasn't flawless; yet he was full of courage to face these creatures.

Damn it.

The skeletons descended the steps, then another two followed. Then three more. In the past, her family's house had crawled with illusions of them.

They teemed into the dungeon as if they'd been poured inside, amassing in front of the demon. The rattle of their bones and snapping of their teeth grew into an agitated din. Scythes scraped the brick walls, sending up sparks.

She yearned to fight, but she had only three battle-magic pouches left. What she wouldn't give for an innate power!

Rök bared his lengthened fangs at them, his face growing harsher with aggression, the planes more demonic. "Come on, I'm waiting for you!" he said, taunting them. "Come to demon."

The gang of skeletons charged, their scythes raised. Rök dodged strikes with uncanny speed and cut through the first wave. Bones flew. Femurs, clavicles, and skulls somersaulted through the air to clatter to the floor.

But they rolled back together to reassemble.

He fended off another wave. They rushed; they fell; they reassembled. So he swung the flat edge of his sword even harder for the next blitz, grunting with effort. He pulverized bones to dust, and the other skeletons held back.

Rök glanced over his shoulder. "See? Just have to hit them hard enough." He winked at her, not knowing that behind him the dust was reforming into bone. "I don't want to label myself a hero of old, but when the shoe fits—"

"Uh, demon?" She jerked her chin in that direction.

He whirled back around. "Huh. New plan." His sword flashed out, crumbling another foe. Before it could reassemble, Rök booted its bones toward an oubliette. The force sucked them down. *Whoosh!*

Clever demon!

He sheathed his sword as another pair charged. Barreling into them, he hoisted one over his shoulder and tossed it to the waiting trap. Dodging another scythe, he grappled to take hold of his next opponent, chucking it in as well.

Bogey after bogey went hurtling toward the oubliettes. Only half a dozen remained.

Yet then a scythe arced toward Rök's face; he blocked the staff with his forearm, just as another scythe caught the backs of his bootheels. He fell backward—right across an oubliette.

"Rök, no!" Would he tumble into nothing, lost forever?

He stiffened his body like a plank. Muscles straining, he resisted the suction and still defended against blows. "I've got this, witch!"

"Hardly!" Poppy snared one of her pouches, power infusing her again. She aimed a beam at the skeleton closest to him, knocking its bones out like bowling pins.

The thing reformed to attack.

Whenever the skeletons swung their scythes, Poppy parried with beams—but they were too fast.

Rök flung himself to the side, just avoiding a strike. The skeleton lost its balance and tumbled skull-first into the abyss. *Whoosh!*

Five left.

Rök repeated the move, tricking another skeleton into the pit. *Four.* Between Poppy's defensive beams and his maneuvering, they took out three more. *Whoosh. Whoosh. Whoosh!*

One left. The demon rocked across the oubliette and yanked his last foe by its ankle bones, sending it bouncing against the sides of the opening. The suction devoured the final skeleton. *Whoosh!*

Enemy defeated.

When Rök rolled to safety, Poppy hastened over, unable to disguise her relief.

Ember and mist filled her senses as he gazed up at her, his eyes glowing even more. Color flushed his cheekbones and his lips curved, tempering his demonic visage. "Are we in the clear?"

She probed the activity of her curse and breathlessly said, "For a bit." Hecate help her, Poppy's desire for him was only growing worse.

Did she want Rök so badly that she would join his rotation of swimbos? Maybe she wasn't as self-respecting as she'd thought. Maybe she was weak where he was concerned.

These fears haunted her as much as her visitors.

When he'd called her the day after their debacle of a date, he'd given no explanation, just asked for a makeup, promising the best steak in all the worlds. So she'd agreed to meet on Halloween, a night when she'd known nothing could tempt her to go, not even Rök. . . .

His grin deepened as he easily made it to his feet. "Look at that worry for me." He brushed his hands off, all cockiness, and not a scratch on him.

Her lips parted as realization hit. "You were never in jeopardy."

"Not even a bit."

"You were playing with them?"

Gleeful nod. "Still consider me mediocre? You actually thought you were riding in to save the day. To save *me*, a demon warrior, from skeletons!"

Her eyes went wide, her face growing hot. "I wasted a pouch on you!"

In a patronizing tone, he said, "Let's consider that magic well spent. I proved my mettle, and I also got a glimpse into your feelings. You do give a damn about me."

"Or maybe I didn't want to feel guilt when my curse killed you."

A flash of doubt crossed his expression. Then his easy smile returned. "Nah. You like me." He reached for her. "This demon's still in the game. Consider your ass mine."

She shoved him into the oubliette.

Whoosh!

SIX

Rök's claws scrabbled along the edge of the hole as he fought the ungodsly suction.

Something I said?

By the time he'd powered his way out, the witch had left him without a glance back. He heard the light tap of her boots as she climbed the stairs.

She knew I could get out of there. Surely, she knew.

He jogged up the steps after her. Okay, maybe he could have been cooler in the moment, but when he'd seen her eyes brimming with concern for him, an uncontrollable thrill had seized him. "Wait up," he called.

Shoulders tense, she strode back in the direction of the foyer.

He followed her out into the spottily lit entryway. "What gives?"

She turned to him with shimmering hands. "You let me waste a pouch on you! Each one takes a day to prepare, and now it will fizzle away to nothing." The light from her palms intensified. "Unless I use it."

"Ah, but you wouldn't, because I'm growing on y—"

Her blast sent him tumbling down the hall. "The hell, witch!" He scrambled to his feet, then loped back to her. "You're out-of-bounds."

"Because it's all a game? Tonight might be a joke to you—a bit of seduction for fun—but this is my life! Now I'm down a pouch with hours left to go."

"You're here to break the curse, aren't you? I can't imagine you'd take bullshit like this lying down."

Her chin rose a notch. Unwilling concession.

"Why here? Did this wizard hex you?" Rök's fangs sharpened again.

"No, he died before the curse struck. But something in this castle is supposed to help me."

"How do you know?"

Exhaling, she lowered her hands, her pique dwindling. He'd learned this witch had a fiery temper, but the storms were quick to pass. "I went to Mariketa the Awaited last week. She tried to sense how to break the curse and came up with one instruction: go to this castle on this night, a lone witch, to find my answer."

"That's it? Fortune cookies say more!"

Poppy sighed and gave him a look: *You're not wrong.*

"Can't you get some other Wiccan to help you?"

"I've tried. I've tried everything."

"If you found out who did this to you, couldn't you force them to lift it?"

"If. *If only.* We've found no trace of whoever did this." She pinched the bridge of her nose. "I first saw a visitor for only an instant. Now they come sunset to sunrise on Halloween, getting stronger and stronger. Soon, they'll start to bleed over into other days. I've plotted the trajectory of *visits*; eventually the nightmares will be constant, and I'll be insane." She gazed up at him. "Or worse. Rök, what if they stay embodied outside the castle? I sense they will. They've got a real taste for it now."

"Then we have to uncover who cursed you. Who are your main suspects? I can help you track them."

"I'm not telling you anything else until you reveal why you're here. Who hired you, and what are you looking for?"

When he hesitated, she said, "What if your job is to find the very thing I need? Mariketa gave me a last piece of advice: *If you find your prize in the castle, don't let them steal it from you.* I thought the tip was strange, because she knows I'm a witch merc; no one steals from me." Poppy raised her hands again, managing a faint glow. "No one."

"I'm not here to steal from you." Recognizing he had no choice but to come clean, he admitted, "I'm only here because of . . . you."

She canted her head. "Why me?"

He scrubbed a palm over his mouth, debating how much of his day he should divulge.

Earlier . . .

Rök sat at the bar in Erol's, phone in his hand, staring at the selfie of him and Poppy from their date. They'd been standing side by side, all but melting into each other, and he'd had the crook of his arm around her neck. Her eyes had been merry, those coral lips curled into a smile.

They looked like they'd taken a thousand such pictures together. Seconds after that snap, they'd been kissing as a warm rain fell.

Gods below, that witch could kiss.

Since then, he'd tried to convince himself he didn't need a

certain red-haired Wiccan in his life. But whenever he saw her now, heat banked inside him. Involuntary smoke would emerge from his fingertips and the ends of his horns.

Humans never would guess that demons had souls. *But we do.*

And Rök believed that Poppy Dyer was the other half of his.

He shoved his phone in his pocket and signaled for another refill, surveying the busy bar. This holiday wasn't usually anything special because every day was Halloween in the Lore. It just meant immortals could move among humans more readily.

With the Accession in full swing, though, everything took on new significance.

Erol's was packed to the rafters with Loreans looking either for hookups—or for power. Couples in the back groped while others huddled over drinks, plotting for an upper hand. Alliances were formed; backs were stabbed; pleasure was had.

Immortals, man.

Tired of it all, he ignored glances from amorous females. The prospect of empty bedsport left him cold, had for years. Resisting the urge to look at that pic again, he wondered how long he'd have before his next awkward summoning.

The bartender, a seal shifter from California, brought over a pitcher of brew, frowning at Rök's empty steel mug.

Apparently, he'd crushed it. He muttered, "Put it on my tab." He needed another job, a truly grueling one to lose himself in.

The shifter gestured to one of Rök's horns and said in a *get-a-grip* tone, "My dude . . ."

"Huh?" Rök reached up and found a piece of his cabin's siding stuck on the tip—from where he'd been ramming his horns against the wall. *Dark gods, the state of me.* He yanked off the wood, crumbling it in his fist.

On a scale from *not fucked up* to *completely fucked up*, Rök was redlining the FU max limit. A demon denied his mate didn't get to be a selfless gentleman. In this strung-out shape, Rök came to a conclusion: *I can't hold out any longer. I need—*

"Poppy."

He jerked his head up when someone mentioned her name.

Not far down the bar, a raven-haired female with flashing eyes poked Deshazior, a demon transporter, in his burly chest. "You'll tell me where you traced her, or I'll permanently blast your demonic testicles right off your demonic body."

It was Poppy's older sister, Lea, a witch so fierce she must channel the Furies. She couldn't find Poppy and was worried, which meant Rök was seriously bloody worried. He'd bet the other Dyer sisters were out combing the city.

Though Lea's threat would make most males quaver, Desh, a storm demon as old as dirt and a former pirate, didn't flinch. He nodded at Lea with understanding, replying in his salty accent: "Wish I could help ye, luv. Don't know a Poppet."

"You bought a pouch from *Poppy* last week! You run the Luber service"—Lore Uber—"and I overheard you two talking about a trip together."

A trip together? Desh was like a bad penny. Rök had laughed when Cade got jealous over Holly's friendship with Desh. Now that storm demon was teleporting around with Poppy in his arms!

Lea snapped, "You'll take me to her now, or I'll GELD you!" Her palms began to glow with magic.

Desh pulled at the collar of his T-shirt, one that read: *Luber Teleporting! No job too small, some jobs too big.* "I got a privacy policy. Can't help ye."

"We'll see, demon." Her raised hands crackled, the rattle before a strike.

In a balls-preserving move, Desh traced away midbeam, leaving his barstool pulverized.

"Damn it!" Lea glared around the room. Immortals, unfazed by the confrontation, shrugged and got back to business.

Rök traced over to her. "What happened to Poppy?"

Lea sneered at him. "Well, if it isn't Rök Kours. I'm surprised your summoners allowed you outside of a bedroom."

He remembered that sneer from the last time they'd talked, when he'd charged over to Poppy's house straight from that restaurant two years ago.

Lea had intercepted him in the yard and had uncannily seen what he'd suspected—that Poppy was his fated one. . . .

Lea raised her glowing palms, threatening him with battle magic. "Poppy might be yours, but you are not hers. *Wiccans don't have mates. What we have is untapped potential and a need for magical protection. When Poppy takes a warlock for her partner, he will unlock her powers, and our entire coven will be strengthened. You can't do that for her. You'll only hobble her for the rest of her life. How selfish are you?"*

"I could protect her." Was he really declaring for Poppy? This was all happening fast. Why wouldn't this witch let him see her?

The light in Lea's palms grew brighter, her expression murderous. "Or you could leave her alone and let her develop her own powers in order to protect *herself. Let me explain this to you simply, demon. You're in a quandary. . . ."*

Now Rök said, "Two years ago you told me about my *quandary*, that if Poppy was my mate and I was decent, I would let her go for her own good." Rök hadn't at first. But after Poppy had stood him up and started seeing that warlock, he'd realized that she likely agreed with her sister.

So for years he'd suffered because he'd wanted to do the right thing by his female. Chaos had been his partner.

No more. Baring his fangs, he said, "Since then, I've accepted two things. Poppy *is* mine. And I am *not* decent." With that, he traced away to search for Desh.

Figuring the storm demon would head to one of his other favorite haunts, Rök teleported to the shadows behind Lafitte's, a low-key bar. Sure enough, Desh was inside, carousing with the humans despite his huge horns. Even outside of Halloween, he mingled with mortals, claiming cosplay for his appearance.

Rök noted he'd changed his T-shirt to one that read: *Big Easy Prosthetics! For every horny occasion!*

"I smell a smoke demon!" Desh called. "Where ye been, Rök? How's Rothkalina these days? I wouldn't know 'cause I haven't transported a single client there. Or anywhere for that matter. I don't even *have* clients! All too private, see?"

Wasting no time, Rök said, "I don't often blackmail, but when I do, I do it quickly." Though Cade always razzed Rök about his spy intrigues, sometimes they worked a trick. "You remember the dirt I uncovered on you?"

Desh swallowed. "What do ye want?"

"For you to trace me to wherever you took Poppy."

"None doing." Desh crossed his beefy arms over his chest. "I'm no angel, mind ye, but I can weather some blackmail more than me business can a privacy violation."

Seeing no other recourse, Rök played the one card all demons would respect.

And Desh bent the rules.

Good thing too. Or Poppy would be dead.

SEVEN

I heard your oldest sister threatening Desh," Rök told Poppy, "demanding to know where he'd taken you. But he wouldn't crack with her. So I decided to come help you out."

"Help *me*?" Great Hecate, this demon confused her!

"Yeah, you. Look, I vow to the Lore I'm not on a job." A vow no immortal could break.

She didn't know what shocked her more: that he hadn't come for a cursebreaker or that he was here solely to help her. He already had. She lowered her hands. "I didn't want to worry Lea, or any of them."

"She strikes me as the type who can handle anything thrown her way, Red."

Mind in overdrive, Poppy headed toward the grand staircase, and he followed. "Since our parents returned to Akelarre, she can be as protective as a mother basilisk over her eggs. She always says, 'We don't have individual burdens. Ours are group burdens. One of the benefits of sisterhood.'" Poppy sighed. "But I don't want to be a burden. And Mariketa did say to come here as a 'lone witch.' So I lied to my sisters about the location of the castle and told them I'd meet them at the house with new information before we set off. That's why I'm under-weaponized. If I'd asked them for help with pouches, they would have known I was setting off on my own." She paused, her brows drawing together. "Desh didn't give my location to Lea. Why would he give it to you?"

"I had some leverage that overrode even his vaunted secrecy, something unquestionable to a fellow demon. Don't ask, because I'm not coming off it. Suffice it to say, I'll be handling your ride out of here."

"I'm going to have a word with him about this."

In a casual tone, Rök asked, "You and he have never . . . ?"

"No. Desh is just a friend." A thought occurred—along with fresh outrage. "You told me you heard something tasty was here, and you wanted to jump all over it!"

Rök waggled his brows at her.

"I don't know if I should be flattered or alarmed that you would risk your life for—lemme check my notes—a kiss? You really want to check this box, huh?"

"I have many plans for your lovely—"

"*Don't.* My gods, doesn't the meaningless scoring ever get old?"

"Can't say it doesn't."

"Then why keep doing it? Why keep racking up members of your swimbo army?"

"I don't have any control over that. It's a smoke demon thing."

"Deciding to sleep with others is entirely in your control."

His lips thinned. "Demons fuck, fight, and revel, right? That's how I'm supposed to pass the centuries. That's what you and everyone else expect from me."

"Yeah. Fuck, fight, and revel. Go, you." What a disappointment he was! She started up the staircase.

Rök clasped her elbow, stopping her. "What else is there

for me to do? How *should* I have spent the last thirteen centuries? You want me to tell you my current existence is empty? It is." He gave off smoke again . . . from frustration? "Waiting for my mate is as bad as you can imagine. I've paced holes in the floor in my cabin, wondering if I'll go mad. I can be in a room packed with Loreans and feel like I've been exiled."

Surprised, she asked, "What do you wish you'd been doing? Settling down? Starting a family?"

"Is that so insane? But I can't do any of that without my mate. I'm supposed to be attempting females to find her, remember?"

That was true. Through sex, a male demon could identify his fated one because he'd be compelled to mark her neck and he would spill his seed inside her. Until that time, he could orgasm with a partner but never experience an ejaculation.

"Chin up, Rök. You might find her this Accession." Then Poppy could stop dwelling on him. She glared at his grip on her arm.

With a reluctant air, he released her. "Older demons keep telling me I'll sense her during an Accession. My first went by with no sign of her. Then my second. Thinking I'd never have her with me was . . . bleak." Did Rök show at all those Lore gatherings because he was *searching*?

If he'd harbored any inkling about Poppy, he would have attempted her instead of remaining with that summoner—someone he knew *wasn't* his mate!

As though he'd read Poppy's thoughts, he said, "Know that what you hate me for . . . I can't help it. You're hating me for being myself."

Why should she expect more from him? He had always been upfront about his rolling-stone, player existence. She was the one wishing he'd change.

When Poppy was little, her mother had told her, "Some things simply aren't meant to be, even for a witch with miraculous powers. Letting go *is* a skill, one more Wiccae could stand to learn."

Poppy had asked, "What if you let go too soon?"

"That's a risk." She'd looked at Poppy quizzically, her green eyes seeming to see far more than merely what was before her. "Sometimes one does have to reach the end. When all is lost, clarity can be found. . . ."

Poppy exhaled, deciding not to give Rök grief for what he couldn't help. Though she saw no future with him, she could work to let go of the past. Clearing her throat, she said, "I don't hate you, Rök. Look, no hard feelings, okay?" She turned to climb the staircase.

He was right beside her, seeming surprised by her words. His mood had shifted again, his smoke dissipating. He acted as if she'd conceded far more than she had. "You fancy a do-over?"

"As friends."

"Hmm." That deep, masculine rumble must be demon for *I disagree but will hold my tongue for now.*

On the landing, they paused before a large portrait of the white-haired wizard in his robes, his wife, and their two kids, a young girl and boy. The wife, dressed in a strapless ball gown and a golden armband, looked wary, as if she'd foreseen how dire her future would prove. Her beringed fingers clutched her children's shoulders.

Some detail about that portrait tickled Poppy's brain. She and Rök both stared at it for long moments.

When they moved on, he rubbed the back of his neck. "Their eyes seem to be following us, don't they?"

Poppy nodded. "Sometimes tropes exist for a reason."

"I'll take a gruesome brawl—innards oozing and hacked-off limbs flying—any day over little jolts of creepiness."

"Then I'm surprised you can stand hanging with me. Witches broker in creepiness."

"Yeah, but your creepy is cute. I'm hexually attracted to you."

She stopped in her tracks. "Oh, my gods, you didn't."

Unrepentant grin. "*Did.* Will do it all night."

Damn it, why'd he have to be fun? She turned to hide her unbidden smile and peered down a hallway lined with doors. It seemed to stretch on forever.

Growing serious, he asked, "How many rooms are there?"

"Over two hundred." Until she found the cursebreaker, she'd have to investigate each one, and the clock was ticking. She imagined nineteen more years of visitors, corporealized now. Her family would try to protect her from these killers, but to what end?

Though her sisters must be furious with her for ditching them tonight, sometimes Poppy went off script. If she survived, she would totally make it up to them, especially Lea.

On the heels of that thought, she wondered what leverage Rök had garnered over Desh. . . .

With a pouch at the ready, she opened the first door. Sheets covered the furniture, the air stuffy. She sensed the area, feeling nothing more than lingering magic. She continued down the hall with Rök at her side to repeat her process in room after room.

Open the door . . . sense the area . . . next.

One room was all purple. One had only a spartan cot on the bare floor. One looked as if it'd been set up for a séance. Another reeked of wolfsbane.

Rök asked her, "Still nothing?"

"Each area gives off a vibe, but I can't puzzle out anything of interest."

"Curious that I haven't scented a hint of the other explorers. What do you know about them?"

"Twenty years ago, six fey archers and a rage demon came here for adventure, never to be heard from again. Their families dispatched the best trackers in the Lore, but no one found a trace of them."

"Maybe I knew the demon." Rök considered himself an honorary rage demon, had told her he felt even more loyalty to that demonarchy than to his own.

"You've probably heard of him. Truller the Victor."

Rök whistled low. "For eons, he won the LoreLympics for strength. I'd heard he disappeared out of the limelight."

"Involuntarily." Researching the previous explorers had almost torpedoed her resolve to come here. When she'd seen a picture of Truller, a tattooed rage demon even bigger than Rök, she'd wondered how she could succeed where that demon—backed by a contingent of fey—hadn't.

But then, she had no choice. She'd come here to safeguard her sanity. Now she was in a battle for her life. Poppy hadn't tasted enough of this existence, the apple uneaten; she would fight on for her future.

Rök said, "If the explorers are withered to husks somewhere inside this castle, I would have scented them."

"Maybe they fell prey to the oubliettes?"

"I didn't detect any trace of a rage demon in the dungeon. No fey either."

"They might have crossed through an invisible rift to another realm and gotten trapped." Poppy was a member of an online forum dedicated to the mysteries of Raven's Murk, and speculation about those explorers was rampant. The "Rift Hypothesis" had gotten a lot of votes.

Rök scratched his chin. "For all we know, gateways like

that could infest this place, and not many other realms are as hospitable as this one. Let me lead." He eased in front of her to open the next door.

Brows raised, she followed.

Gateways to other realms. More visitors. A ticking clock . . . Much was on the line.

So why couldn't she drag her gaze off Rök's muscular back, outlined by his well-worn shirt? Her earlier resolution to let him go was already faltering. Her body wasn't ready. Because her body was indeed a fucking idiot.

She'd always found it humorous when imperiled movie characters got distracted by sex. But maybe the lurking threats explained *why* Poppy's attraction to Rök had reached stratospheric levels. Maybe physical danger called to mind other physical things.

Plus, he was temptation incarnate.

"Ah, witch," he said, satisfaction in his tone. "I can feel your eyes on me. The chemistry between us is as undeniable as ever."

But chemistry was all it would ever be with him. And it hadn't been enough to lure him back to her on their date. Which made her wonder how strong it'd been with the temptress who'd summoned him that night.

He turned to Poppy. "If we could bottle it, neither of us would have to take a job again."

"Oh, you want to retire but can't? Haven't saved enough coin?"

His eyes smoldered. "Just waiting for my rainy day."

The feeling of connection she'd first experienced on their date bloomed again. Before then, they had worked in the same field, passing each other with preoccupied waves, but that night, she'd felt he really *saw* her.

Not so.

Yet she'd had that same connected feeling last year at a big Lore bonfire. She'd spotted him talking to a few gorgeous sirens. Without warning, he'd turned to Poppy, catching her eye over a crowd of rowdy immortals.

As she and Rök stared at each other, the crowd had faded away until she could almost hear his heartbeat. She'd spied smoke rising from his skin and had wanted it to surround her. *Yes, connection.*

He'd mouthed something to her, but she couldn't make out the words. Then the scantily clad sirens had tried to reclaim his attention, reminding her that he had an actual connection— a summoning pact!—with many. She'd portaled away before he could see her crestfallen expression.

Since then, trying to figure out what he'd said had driven her crazy. She could ask him, but doubted he'd remember. In any case, Poppy had too much on her plate to ponder that or his odd behavior. She certainly would never ask what that summoner had over her. "Focus, demon."

"Very well." Grinning, he moved to the next room. "No idea what we might be searching for?"

That *we* did funny things to her. "I pictured the cursebreaker as some kind of talisman, but it could be anything. I've seen enchanted shrimp forks and bespelled golf clubs before."

"Whatever it is, we'll find it."

We.

Hecate help her, she basked in this attention. She relished his presence. She was just mercenary enough to appreciate the help of a free bodyguard.

If a bull never caught a red cape, would he chase it forever?

Rök closed the latest door, saying, "A thought occurred to me. You scheduled our second date on Halloween, the night of your curse. You never intended to show." His expression was studiously blank.

"No, I didn't. And you were put off readily enough, so it worked out for everyone."

"Hmm. Maybe you insisted on that night because you were afraid you *would* meet me."

How easily he saw through her. "Rök, I told you I'm looking for a relationship. I want something I can depend on. Maybe a family." Even though Wiccae didn't have fated mates, Poppy understood the power of a pure, abiding love; her parents had been together happily for half a millennium.

I want what they have. Had she thought Ixius could give her everything she yearned for? No. Looking back, she feared she'd used him to make her family happy while distracting her from what could never be.

Her gaze was unerringly drawn to the demon.

"A relationship, then? I'll throw my hat into the ring." Teasing her yet again. "What do you like in a bloke? I mean, besides not asking stupid fucking questions."

"My bar isn't high. He'd have to be honest and loyal and *not* fated to someone else. I won't be a placeholder." *I won't!*

"Well, it is an Accession," Rök said in a noncommittal tone. "Maybe you'll find him soon."

"Maybe."

A weird frisson of tension tangled between them, but it faded as they continued their search.

"So what have you been up to over the last pair of years?" he asked.

Jobs. Spinning my wheels in a doomed relationship. Still living down my disastrous date with you. She kept it light. "Recently our cat Newt drank a transmogrification potion and turned into a dog for a week. Now she barks, slobbers, and humps the legs of the unwary." Poppy lapped up Rök's laughter like Newt with an unsupervised potion. "What have you been up to?"

"I moved out of the pool house I'd shared with Cade and found a new place, but I spend as much time as I can at his and Holly's house. The twins can trace anywhere they've been before, so the three of us do a lot of search missions. One time we found the girls at the Valkyries' new lair. Holly's aunts were playing toss-the-babies with the girls, who were delighted. Mom, Dad, and Uncle Rök were less so. . . ."

As Poppy and Rök searched, conversation flowed, nearly as comfortable and natural as on their date. She tried to plumb his mood and got the impression that he was excited about spending time with her. But she also sensed . . . relief.

Strange demon. They kept the topics light, though she itched to know what had really happened to him since their date. Why had he booked so many jobs practically guaranteed to get even an immortal merc killed?

After checking all the rooms on this floor, they followed the hall to a stairwell. Inside, they gazed up and up and up.

Rök said, "I didn't see this many stories from the outside. The exterior must be an illusion."

"Or this is." Up the stairs they went to the next floor and another seemingly endless corridor with dozens of doors. "Searching will take hours." Poppy glanced at her watch. Time continued to slip past.

"I have an idea," Rök said dryly. "We should split up."

Despite everything, a chuckle escaped her. His expression was lively, his smile mesmerizing. Gods, she wished she could get over him. The sight of him like this was another memory she'd store, never to be erased.

"How do you eat an elephant, witch? Bite by bite."

"Do demons eat elephants?"

"Just a human saying. Demons aren't so different from Wiccae."

"I would beg to differ, but I never beg." Despite what he'd fantasized. *Beg* more *until she begged* no more.

How . . . intriguing.

"Hmm." That deep rumble washed over her, penetrating her defenses. The comfort between them evaporated, scorched away by sexual tension. "You give a demon ideas, Poppy. When we get out of here, I'm going to . . ." His unfinished promise hung in the air, his gaze narrowing on her eyes. "Glowing again. Looks like we're in for more adventures."

Only then did she notice the curse churning. Somewhere in this castle, a child's laughter rang out.

EIGHT

The hair on the back of Rök's neck had stood up a split second before he heard a kid's laugh. Yet that taunting sound was nothing like the twins' bubbly giggles.

When Poppy turned down the hallway, he said, "So we're just going to ignore that laughter?" He opened the closest door.

She sensed the room. "Sometimes I'll hear the visitors but won't see them. Maybe I won't have to tangle with that particular nightmare tonight."

"*We* won't have to." He checked his mental database of horror movie villains. "So are we talking about a killer doll?"

"Depends. Do you smell corn?"

"No."

"Then it's a doll."

"Fantastic."

"Things are always fantastic with you."

He raised his brows. "Better than saying *that's fucked* with each of your revelations."

Instead of taking offense, she nodded as if he'd made a good point.

More laughter sounded. Years ago, he'd overheard humans talking about a killer doll movie. One had commented, "What a demonic little shit."

Rök recalled being offended. *Demonic, my ass.* He'd been tempted to show them his demon self. Now he asked Poppy, "If it shows, how do we kill it? Burn or behead?" He hoped the latter. This dusty carpet could catch fire and spread, and the castle wasn't exactly filled with emergency exits.

"Sometimes . . . more than one doll shows up."

"Let me guess: each one has to be killed in a different way?"

"Though this is a new situation for me, my research indicates so. But one of them—Annelise—can't be killed at all, which is a problem since she's telekinetic. Just be careful if you see them."

He opened another door. "If I'm not, I know you'll protect me, like you did with those skeletons. You cried, 'I'll save you!' and hustled into the fray for me. How adorable was that?"

Her lips quirked.

Imitating her voice, he said, "Never fear, my precious demon! I'll muster all my magic against these foes to defend you!"

She lost the battle and fully smiled. Spellbinding witch. "You finished?"

"Never." He leaned in beside her ear and whispered, *"BOO!"*

She laughed, a throaty sound that made him want to rub his horns all over her. "Okay, okay."

"You pitted me against gremlins, skeletons, and now I might have to face . . . *dollies.*"

Her amusement faded. "Don't underestimate them, Rök."

"If I get taken out by a doll, then I deserve it, yeah? I'm still waiting for a challenge." On to the next room . . . "For that matter, if we run into trouble again, save your pouches for your own protection. How many do you have left?"

She'd probably never given an arsenal inventory to another merc before. Indicating a measure of trust, she said, "Two for battle magic and one for a portal."

That was it? He felt guilty that she'd blown one on the skeletons.

She gazed ahead, so many thoughts going on behind those eyes. Heavy thoughts.

To distract her, he said, "Hey, vampires, werewolves, and witches used to be popular Halloween fodder for mortals. Do you ever get them as visitors? They could give us an actual fight."

"A few decades ago, I saw a lot of them, but they corresponded more to humans' ideas of us. Think green-skinned witches, snouty werewolves covered in fur, and caped vamps with chin-length fangs."

"Demons?"

Her eyes glimmered, his merry witch returned. "Small with pointy tails and pitchforks."

"Ouch! So your visitors are creatures that humans *believe* are myths—except some of them are real? Well, that just complicates the Lore needlessly, no?"

"Keeps things interesting." Another bright grin. How had he ever considered her looks anything less than exquisite?

The children's laughter sounded once more, this time accompanied by the eerie tip-tap of little shoes.

The sconce to his right flared; something shifted to his left. He yanked free his sword and pivoted in that direction—

Only to confront his own game face, reflecting back from a large wall mirror.

With a relieved exhalation, he sheathed his blade. "Jump scare, huh?" He admired his reflection and smoothed his hair. "No wonder you can't keep your eyes off me. Was there ever a more smokin' smoke demon?"

She snorted. "Your sizable ego must be visible from the Elserealms."

"Not the only part of me that can make such a claim." He casually looped his arm around her neck, gazing at her in the mirror. "And you, pretty as a picture."

Her cheeks heated at the compliment. She seemed to melt against him, just as she'd done in that parking lot.

"Speaking of pictures, do you ever pull up that selfie we took?" He'd sent it to her before she'd blocked him.

Her gaze flicked away. "I kind of deleted it."

She was telling the truth. "I see." His shot with her felt more and more distant. Was he not "romantic partner" material? He'd hoped she was different from the females who summoned him over the centuries, the ones who'd dismissed him afterward with all the care they'd give an overworked vibrator. Did Poppy view him the same way? She might've gone out with Rök just to scratch an itch.

Maybe she was so hard-core Wiccan that she would never consider a demon for more.

With nothing to lose, he bluffed her: "You deleted the pic because you stared at it as much as I've stared at my copy. You scheduled our makeup date on Halloween night so you wouldn't give in to the urge to meet me."

"Aww. Poor addled demon. You're delusional with your advanced age."

Not a denial. He grasped her hand, marveling anew at her soft skin. "After we took that selfie, we turned toward each other for a kiss, like we'd been together for ages. We both knew we'd kiss. We both knew it'd wreck us. It was as inevitable as dawn. Just like now."

Her breath hitched.

Dark gods below, he wanted her. "Your last kiss seared me.

Left a mark on me forever." He pressed his lips against her wrist and flicked her pulse point with his tongue, like he'd done on their date.

She watched him with fascination, murmuring, "You are all temptation, aren't you?"

"I *am* a demon."

"And in exchange for your protection you only asked for a mere kiss." She was playing with him, and he was going to let her! "Maybe I could give you a down payment."

"I should have asked for more."

"Then earn a tip."

"Fucking hell, witch, you drive me crazy." When uncontrollable smoke rose from his body, her heartbeat quickened, a light drum in his ears. "I can hear your reaction to me."

"I can *see* yours."

He palmed her nape and dragged her closer. "Because you make me burn." He covered her lips with his own, savoring her sharp inhalation. He gave her a moment, expecting her to pull away.

He groaned when she didn't. Cupping her face and tilting his head, he slanted his mouth over hers, delving for her taste. She was confection-sweet, addictive. He flicked her tongue with his, and she moaned as she met him. The entire world coalesced into that contact.

Tongues twining . . . trading moans and groans . . . wrapping his arms around her irresistible body. This kiss wasn't as good as the night of their date.

Better.

He should concentrate on the danger, but demonic drives battled inside him: to protect his mate and to pleasure her. He reached for her hair tie and released it, threading his fingers through those silken locks as he deepened the kiss.

She dug her nails into his back, meeting him stroke for stroke. Lost in this woman, he cupped her breast, thumbing her stiffened nipple, lightly pinching it. Her gasp made his cock surge in his pants. He wanted it buried to the hilt inside her, his female claimed.

Possessiveness seethed within him when his lusty witch writhed to get closer, rubbing her curves against him. The scent of her arousal hit him like a drug. *Poppy . . .*

Gods, she was ready to mate—

A twisting pain zinged him in the side, and he jerked back. "Damn, Red. I'm not down with pinching." She'd all but torn his skin, cooling his ardor.

She frowned. "I didn't pinch you." Her irises glowed even more.

"If you didn't . . . ?"

Their attention dropped to the bottom corner of the mirror; glassy eyes stared up at them.

Rök tossed Poppy behind him.

Standing in the hall was a porcelain doll with blond ringlets and a frilly dress.

A pent-up laugh escaped him. "A mirror scare, too! Next we'll meet cave creatures and unearth found footage."

She moved to his side and whispered, "Oh, Hecate, no. This isn't funny."

A walking doll? "It's a little funny."

"That's *Annelise*."

The doll blinked those glassy eyes at Poppy, then swiveled its head to face Rök.

Just because the situation amused him didn't mean it couldn't also be disturbing. "Wiggins activated, huh?"

Poppy grabbed his hand. "Back away. Then *run*."

"Not a chance. My centuries of Lore cred would get revoked if I run from a toy."

"She's not a toy. She's a demonic entity."

"So am I." He winked at Poppy.

"Please, Rök. She's the telekinetic one."

"I can lift a building. Her telekinesis can't outmatch my strength. It'll take more than this doll to bring me down after all these years. . . ." He sensed a new threat at his back. He yanked Poppy behind him again and whirled around.

Three more dolls stood not ten feet before him. He recognized the maniacal, red-haired one with the long, serrated blade, but not the pair of miniature mannequin-looking things.

He rolled his eyes. He didn't have time for this bullshit, was gaining ground in his mission to win Poppy. Seduction was only the first step.

He brandished his sword and struck with supernatural speed. *Slash.* His aim was true, yet they'd disappeared.

Laughter and tip-tapping sounded behind him. With Poppy close, he twisted around and found the four dolls lined up, eight creepy eyes staring at him. He lunged and lopped off the head of one of the mannequin dolls. Its weird body collapsed. "One down."

Yet then it rose. Skipped to its severed head. And *reattached* it.

"Huh."

Just as Rök struck again, the Annelise doll raised her arm. The air rippled. He gaped when his feet left the ground; then he and Poppy were launched down the hall.

Annelise slammed them against a far wall, knocking the breath from Poppy's lungs. The doll pinned her and Rök there like insects.

Can't get free! Poppy's vision wavered as she struggled.

Annelise could twist their heads off at any time—true immortal deaths. With that awareness, Poppy's life did indeed flash before her eyes.

Her parents' proud smiles. Her sisters laughing. The pungent smell of herbs and the bite of a brewing concoction.

Rök's sinful grin and bad jokes. His scorching kisses.

She fought to crane her head toward him. They met gazes.

"Poppy!" He looked frantic for her, his blue eyes turning gray, reflex smoke emerging from his skin.

Annelise used her power to pry his sword from his clenched fingers and cast it away. Then she threw him to the floor as if *he* were a rag doll.

"Rök, no!"

Annelise telekinetically pinned him while the others leapt atop his sprawled body. One's serrated blade plunged toward his chest.

Rök managed to block it. "Fucker!" But he couldn't get loose.

"Leave him alone!" Poppy strained against Annelise's force to reach her bag.

"Get free and run," Rök grated. He missed a block; the blade stabbed, coming up bloody. The maniacal doll leered with delight.

"I'm not leaving you!"

With another wave of her arm, Annelise began to strangle Rök. His disbelieving face turned purple. Veins bulged in his temples.

The whites of his eyes burst red as the blade plunged again. Rök's blood spurted. The mannequins were covered in it, battering his head and horns with glee.

Poppy screamed, "Stop!" She couldn't reach a pouch, and he was running out of oxygen. If he couldn't defend, they would take his head.

Rök. Gone forever.

When all is lost, clarity is found. Three realizations hit Poppy. What was at stake. What she coveted. What she feared—

Rök somehow thrashed his mighty body to the side. He'd loosened Annelise's hold!

His move must've startled the doll, interrupting her telekinesis; Poppy was able to snag a pouch, receiving the magic. She freed her arm enough to fire on Annelise. "Get away from him, you bitch!" Magic shot from her.

The doll fired back with one hand, resuming her hold on Rök with her other.

Poppy's continuous beam battled Annelise's telekinesis— one force blazing, one invisible. The stalemate drained Poppy's strength like water through a colander. *I'm fighting her. I'm fueling her. Fighting myself.* Her beam sputtered to nothing, yet Annelise too seemed weakened.

Rök managed to beat away the others, tossing them down the hall!

With the tide turning, Poppy yelled and freed herself from the wall. She ran to Rök just as he staggered to his feet.

When the dolls gathered for another attack, Rök yanked Poppy behind him, roaring, "Let off, you little pricks!"

Suddenly they . . . did, backing away. Had Annelise cocked her head to listen for something approaching?

How could dolls even hear? *Because they fucking can.*

Rök glanced back at her. "You okay?"

Shaky nod. "We have to get out of here."

HISSSSSS. StStSt. HISSSSSS.

"What's that hissing, witch?"

Poppy knew that sound.

The aliens had come.

NINE

Five new nightmares loped down the hall. The sparse light reflected off their black exoskeletons and dripping fangs. With each hiss, viscous liquid drizzled from their two mouths.

Annelise gave a curtsy to the newcomers; then she and the other dolls disappeared.

Rök rushed to secure his sword, placing himself between Poppy and the new threat. He sucked in a breath as he raised his weapon. That redheaded doll had stabbed him through twice, barely missing his heart.

The five monsters readied, their massive heads bobbing left to right, their tails flicking. They were bigger than he'd thought they might be. *Serves me right for rewatching on my phone.* He glanced over his shoulder. "So when you said aliens, you meant *aliens.*"

Wide-eyed, Poppy said, "Uh-huh. I've seen them before but never quite like this."

"For blood, they have—"

"Oh, yeah."

Would spatter ignite the carpet? At the very least, slashing them would dissolve his sword. With reluctance, he sheathed the weapon that had seen him through two Accessions, his confidence that he could keep Poppy safe taking a hit.

What if Lea had been right about her sister needing more than a demon? His protective instincts were primed as never before, both amping and terrifying at the same time: *I'll annihilate whatever threatens Poppy; what if I . . . can't?*

He reminded himself that he'd somehow stayed away from his mate for two years, so he figured he could do anything. "I'll hold them off. Run."

"You can't teleport or travel through your smoke. You can't use your sword. Don't be an idiot."

"I think the phrase you're looking for is *godsdamned demonic hero.*" He eyed their foes for vulnerabilities. *I can snap their necks. If I can reach them.*

Poppy's hand darted into her bag for another pouch. "I've got this."

"Conserve your ammo. That's your last battle magic, right?"

"You needed my help against the dolls, and you need it again now."

"I was wearing them down!"

"By being stabbed?"

"Exactly." His wounds hurt, but he would regenerate. "Just save your pouch."

The aliens charged; a beam zoomed past him, bombarding them. *She didn't save her pouch.*

Their bodies hurtled backward, injured. Smoke rose from the carpet, but it didn't ignite. This time.

Over his shoulder, Rök said, "No spatter! We can't risk a fire."

"Then run with me!"

"I can handle them." As they rebounded, he drew on his dark half, turning demonic. His body grew hazy, his muscles swelling. He bared his lengthening fangs, roaring a warning.

The aliens didn't heed it, attacking as a unit. Tails stabbed at him like sword strikes as he evaded. Their strength and speed was more than supernatural. Magic-infused?

But he was a warrior at the peak of his powers. He dodged swiping claws to grab one's unwieldy head. He twisted it till pressure gave way, its neck broken.

SNAP.

The body hadn't even collapsed before he'd seized the next alien, dodging its secondary maw to grapple for its head. The demon in him craved mindless slaughter, but Rök had learned to control his primal self. He studied, reflected, and adjusted, all with a demon's aggression.

SNAP.

Ah. He'd figured out their weakness, the pattern revealing itself. *Strategy.* All that remained was implementation.

Dodging. Grappling. Twisting.

Five aliens soon lay vanquished at his feet, with none of their blood spilled. He'd defended his mate, had the impulse to plant his boot atop a corpse and pound his chest with a bellow.

"You took them all out, Rök." The way she gazed up at him as if in awe . . .

He would do *anything* for more of that look. "We can best these creatures. Now that they're embodied, we can kill them all." Had he made her feel a thread of hope about the future? Rök, though not a warlock, could help her prevail against a mystical curse.

Doubt clouded her expression. "There's too many. Human nightmares are limitless."

"Bite by bite, yeah? We'll drop them one at a time." As soon as he'd spoken, he sensed movement behind him.

What now? One alien's spindly fingers clenched and unclenched. Another's tail circled about like a cracked whip.

They began to rise, no worse for the wear.

That was bloody unexpected. "New plan. We need to get them to the dungeon. I can send them to hell—" The skeletons from earlier materialized behind the aliens.

Which meant the visitors *couldn't* be killed or even cast away. How to defeat an enemy that would forever rebound?

Poppy spoke his thoughts: "We can't fight creatures that refuse to die. *Now* will you run with me?"

He glanced at their foes readying to attack, then back at her. Cursing in Demonish, he grabbed her arm, and they fled down the hall.

The aliens alone gave chase. Three dogged their heels while another pair launched themselves onto the ceiling to clamber along at full speed.

Rök and Poppy careened around a corner, turning into a narrower corridor. No doors or windows. Just the same worn carpet beneath their feet.

The aliens closed in, gaining speed.

"Faster, witch!" Rök shoved her in front of him, pushing her along. Snapping jaws and swiping claws just missed him. "Go, go, go!"

When they came to a fork in the hallway, he lifted her in his arms and sprinted as if there were a run on demon brew. After what felt like miles passed beneath his feet, he glanced over his shoulder. He'd managed some breathing room.

Was the best move to find the cursebreaker at all costs or locate the battery and escape this place, living to fight another day? His instincts urged him to remove Poppy from harm's way.

The feel of her delicate body clasped against him heightened his resolve. He'd do whatever it took to protect her—even from herself. He ran harder, barreling down corridors, pulling farther away from their pursuers. He reached a second fork. Turned right. Another fork. Right. Then left. Then right.

The aliens' clambering grew faint. They'd chosen the wrong direction!

At last, the end of the hall loomed with a door that looked as if it'd come from a medieval castle. Spikes jutted around the door lever, warning them away.

Poppy whispered, "The hell is this?"

In the distance, the aliens hissed. After a beat, their steps thundered in Rök and Poppy's direction.

"No choice." He pulled on the lever. Instead of opening, the door began to vibrate. Whirring gears and sliding bolts sounded, like a bank vault opening.

The aliens turned the corner.

"They're coming!" Poppy's hand dove into her satchel. "I'll create a portal to another part of the castle."

He yanked on the lever. "We're not there yet. I'll tell you when I need help."

Bogeys fifteen feet away.

Ten . . .

The door opened. Rök tossed Poppy inside and slammed the heavy door behind them. The aliens shoved back, claws pinging the spikes. A secondary maw extended through the growing gap in the doorway. *Snap snap!*

"Push, demon!" Poppy leaned in beside him, using her own immortal strength to help. "I should've made a puddle out of them, huh?"

He grated, "Can't risk a fire."

Snap snap!

"You'd rather an alien bite off your head?"

Claws replaced the maw, those spindly fingers stretching. . . .

Rök gritted his fangs and shoved as hard as he could,

utilizing all his demonic brawn. Just before the edge of the door sliced the alien and sent spatter everywhere, it retreated. Rök and Poppy slammed the door closed.

Outside, the hissing and strikes faded as those same gears whirred, bolts clanking—a sprung trap.

Between breaths, Poppy said, "That doesn't sound good."

He noticed what looked like a steam-punk combination lock on the door—and blood all over its surface. "It locks from the inside. Sitrep, witch." They whirled around.

She muttered, "Well, hell."

TEN

Poppy and the demon had entered a room as big as a warehouse.

The scent of formaldehyde stung her nose as she surveyed their new surroundings. Flickering sconces and lightning lit the vast space sporadically, leaving shadowy alcoves. Layers of cobwebs covered haphazard stacks of books.

Above them, rain pounded against a glass dome inlaid with metal bars. A lightning rod protruded from its center. Wires descended from it to branch out like veins through what appeared to be a laboratory.

Some of those wires ran to multiple tanks atop shelves. They looked like cylindrical aquariums, only these were filled with green goo—and body parts.

"I'm getting some mad, mad-scientist vibes." Despite the alien threat in the hall, Rök yanked on the door latch, but it didn't budge. "Did the wizard lock his lab from the inside to keep something in?"

She nodded. "Judging by the blood on the door, whatever it was wanted out."

"Why not just magically barricade this place behind him?"

"It must be a redundancy. Which means we're trapped within a trap." The bars in the dome made this place look like a giant cage.

Rök glanced up. "Maybe it's not completely sealed. I might be able to bust through those bars and have us out of here in time for cocktails. Be right back for you." He leapt the forty or so feet up to punch the dome. His fist recoiled, and he dropped right back down. "Bloody boundary spell."

"It surrounds every inch of this place."

"Fantastic." Once all grew quiet outside the door, he glanced at her eyes. "The glow is muted. When are more of your visitors going to show?"

"It feels like I'm in a lull, but not a good one. I get the sense that their next visit will be like a tsunami of shit coming my way."

"*Our* way," he said, swiping blood from a horn. "I can't believe we just faced off against dolls and aliens." Not to mention those reappearing skeletons. Rök must be wondering how he and Poppy could possibly survive the night. "You have any blast power left?"

She shook her head. "I'm fueling the magic in those pouches but also the visitors. Every time they attack, their outlay takes a toll on me."

"Once I find out who cursed you, I'll torture them for centuries on end—teaching them the meaning of agony."

Even as Rök's ruthless words charmed her, she felt a murderous heat toward whatever foe had done this to her. "You'll have to get in line."

Rök turned back to the lock pad, trying to jimmy it open, but it proved as impenetrable as everything else. "Can you pick this? Wicca it up."

"I told you—I only have my portal spell left."

"No innate witchly powers? You've got to have something outside of your bag."

I have nothing! Poppy was only as good as her pouch count. "I'm not a safecracker. Even if I had that talent, the wizard's power was stronger than mine could ever be."

"Okay, okay." Rök assessed the area. "This lab is huge. The castle's battery could be in here."

"Or it could be in Poughkeepsie. Magic doesn't often work like electricity." So much voltage crackled in this place, her loosened hair felt like it stood on end. Or maybe her earlier realizations were spooking her.

What was at stake: *That these embodied visitors will keep coming till they kill me and everyone I love.*

What she coveted: *A life free of them with a partner who loves and respects me.*

What she feared: *That I'll accept anything less—or die before I get a chance at that life.*

"Even if we found the battery, I can't leave," she told him. "Not until my mission is complete."

Seeming to choose his words carefully, he said, "With all these vantages and blind corners, this lab will be a kill zone if your visitors reappear in here. We might actually be in trouble."

She nodded. "Yes. And you should go if you can. I don't want you to get hurt. But for my part, if I return home empty-handed, I'll jeopardize my sisters." She would do anything to protect them, just as they would do anything for her—including putting themselves in danger.

Fierce Lea would charge into the line of fire with a battle cry, studious Sage and mischievous Clove right behind her. Lethal Bella would fight to the death for just about any cause, but especially for Poppy.

"Rök, if I don't find a way to stop the visitors, I sense that they will kill me and those I love. They won't quit till we're all dead."

He appeared to wrestle with his thoughts. At length, he said, "Do you think the cursebreaker is in here?"

"Maybe?" She had to believe the answer was close.

Both of their gazes settled on an area in a far corner of the lab, one concealed behind an oversize curtain. *Never a good sign.*

He said, "We're going behind that curtain, aren't we?"

"Yep."

"Not going to like what we see?"

"Nope."

"Nothing ventured, huh. Just stay close, okay?" He started in deeper, using his enhanced sight to scan the shadows.

As they walked, she ignored the ancient spider eggs crunching beneath their boots and regarded his wounds. The doll's blade had stabbed him through. "You were really hurt."

"I'll be fine." He shrugged his broad shoulders, then winced.

His pain called to her, and she had to ball her fists to keep from touching him. "At least you're regenerating quickly." His eyes had already healed from the starbursts of red.

He gave a short laugh. "Am I, then?"

Sympathy elicited honesty. "If I don't get another chance to tell you . . . I have heard all about your exploits, and they aren't mediocre."

He gave her a questioning look, as if she might be teasing him again.

"Even before tonight, I recognized how well you fight." She'd been agog at his skill with a sword, his style a mix of demon brutality and cold precision. *Fire and ice.* "And your intel is next-level. Everyone knows that."

"Thanks, Red. I appreciate it. I wish I'd gotten to do research on this place. Not knowing the ins and outs is throwing me." He hadn't had a chance because he'd rushed to her side.

"I'm a member of a forum that speculates on the mysteries surrounding Raven's Murk. It's a great place to exchange information, except for the literal trolls. They somehow found their way online. Anyway, the message boards contain a ton of details about this castle and the wizard. A lot of it is conjecture, but some has been proven correct."

"Did those forum members predict this?" Rök waved at their surroundings.

"Could anyone have?"

As they passed the tanks with body parts, he swore low. "This lab couldn't get any creepier."

Lightning struck the rod at that moment, the glare blinding them. Electricity buzzed, traveling down the wires to those tanks. One severed leg juddered, the foot kicking the glass with a watery *thud thud thud.*

"It just did." The portrait on the landing flashed into her thoughts. "I'm starting to suspect what the wizard was doing here."

"Don't say *the reanimation of corpses.*"

She sighed. "Totally the reanimation of corpses." *Thud thud thud.* "He wanted to resurrect his wife and children."

"Fantastic!"

"You really have a problem with dead things coming back to life."

"You've discovered my no-longer-secret weakness," Rök said. "He must've been keeping his subjects in that dungeon."

They'd discovered the answer to another mystery: the wizard had indeed turned balls-out evil. "Then he was as horrific as my visitors."

Rök frowned at her. "At our dinner, you never mentioned your curse, even though we discussed monsters."

"Not something I lead with on a first date."

He kicked an empty crate out of their way. "You tell that warlock of yours?"

"Ixius and I shared more than a first date."

Rök's jaw muscles bulged. Jealousy from the demon? *Delicious.*

She'd told Ixius because she'd thought he could help her. But warlocks were tricky, and good ones like her father were rare.

Most hated witches, were intimidated by their feminine strength. Others wanted to siphon off a witch's power, while giving nothing in return.

Skewing toward the latter, Ixius had been disappointed when Poppy failed to manifest any abilities. In the end, she'd been well rid of him.

Rök said, "When I asked you that night why you thought humans liked horror movies, you got a strange look on your face and told me, 'Because it feels like a near miss. And in the face of death, life is even more precious.'"

"I remember," she said, surprised he did.

"You were speaking from experience. Every Halloween your life becomes a horror movie."

"Now yours has too." A veil of web wafted over her. She scrubbed her face, spitting against the strands. *Pfft!*

This entire castle was a web, and she'd flown right into it, dragging Rök in as well. *Thanks, Mariketa.* How could Poppy keep fighting to find the cursebreaker? How could she not? "I'll bet you've never gone through this much trouble to get laid. You must be regretting your decision to come here."

His gaze drifted to her lips. "Worth it just for that kiss."

Her heart sped up from the memory, and judging from his sidelong grin, he heard it. "Oh, come on, Rök. That's a steep downside for a kiss. We've got hours to go, and more unkillable visitors will come."

"You'd be dead if I hadn't hitched a ride here with Desh. So I have zero regrets. Remember, I'm not concerned about me. I just want to keep you safe."

So she hadn't imagined the worry in his eyes when Annelise had struck. Despite Poppy and Rök's history, the demon truly cared about her. "Why is it your job to keep me safe?"

"You hired my sword."

"Now you've been paid. But you won't be happy with one kiss."

"No." He gazed down at her. "I won't."

Or maybe the player just wanted to check this box. *Ugh.*

Thud thud thud. That sound needled her; his attitude grated. Soon irritation hummed inside her like the electricity all around. She was pissed to be trapped here, pissed that some asshole somewhere had cursed her. She was super pissed that the demon still affected her like this.

Over the course of a years-long rivalry, one horrendous date, and a perilous castle jaunt, had she ceded a piece of her heart to him?

What if she never got it back? He'd given her another kiss that had turned her inside out, with the promise of nothing more. His *kiss* was a curse.

Which meant she'd been doubly cursed.

More webs ghosted over her. *Pfft.* Spider eggs cracked beneath her boots. Lightning forked out. That leg went *thud thud thud.* Everything about this place charged her temper.

Rök looked like he suffered the same, his shoulder muscles bunching. In a curt tone, he asked, "Are you dead set on dating a warlock?"

"What are you talking about?"

"You told your ex that you'd bring a hundred *other warlocks* to the table."

She'd just been keeping with the theme. "Why are my dating standards any of your business? At least I knew he wouldn't get summoned."

"Standards, is it? And one more time, I can't help summonings."

"You can break your pact with females." *Thud thud thud.* "Admit it: you don't want to."

"I don't go out of my way to hurt them. Once I claim my mate, all this will take care of itself. They know I'll never stray from her."

I know this too! So why was Poppy even looking at him? "You can't convince me that you don't love the attention. The *need.* You love it, or else you would stop it." *Thud thud thud. Pfft. IRRITATION.* "Why did you have to be such a big disappointment?"

He whirled around on her. "Because I'm a demon and demon things happen? You're a disappointment too—hating me for things I can't control!"

Danger, attraction, and that wild electricity charged them up like lightning desperate to strike. Words left her lips: "What was so special about the woman who summoned you from our date? Was she sexier than me?" Poppy's voice broke with emotion. "A better kisser?"

"Are you high? No one's sexier to me. No one's a better kisser. Gods, witch, you nearly made me come in my pants in the parking lot!"

She drew her head back in confusion. "Then why didn't you return to me? *Why?*" Her voice cracked on the word, but she was beyond caring.

"I did come back, and you were gone. I told you I sometimes temporarily disappear, was honest about it. You knew I might get summoned, and you still ditched!"

"I waited for an hour!"

"Because I'm a demon, and you don't want a . . ." He frowned. "I wasn't gone an hour."

"That's when I left, so it was longer. But hey, males tend to lose track of time if they're balls deep. Did you give a single thought to me, sitting alone in that restaurant?"

Frustration evaporating, he quietly said, "I didn't think I'd been gone that long."

"Explain the situation to me. A woman you used to sleep with summoned you because she needed a chess partner? Or some furniture moved? Or, more likely, for sex."

Lips thinned, he turned to check behind the door of a storage cabinet. "That's all I ever get summoned for. I serve a function: empty, emotionless sex."

"You resent that?"

"Maybe. But I understand it. Everybody knows I'm destined for my mate, so no one wants anything more." He faced her. "The fact remains: Poppy, I didn't bed anyone that night."

"Then what took an hour? Did you get caught in a time warp?" Cadeon had gotten caught in one with a beautiful demoness, leading Holly to suspect the worst.

Rök shook his head. He parted his lips to speak, then seemed to think better of what he'd been about to say. Finally he muttered, "I got summoned again. And again. Maybe a few times after that. Erol's must've been running a drink special or something. And it *was* a Saturday night."

"Oh, Hecate, what a piece of work! You're like a debauched pinball bouncing around from one score to the next." And she'd dared to consider placing herself into the rotation?

"I didn't sleep with anyone!" Could that possibly be true? "I made my usual excuses, but extricating myself takes time. More than I figured, I guess. Being summoned isn't like teleporting. It's a mind fuck. I never know where I'll appear. I get taken from a dead sleep or right when I sit down to a meal I'm looking forward to. And then that night with you, everything was perfect. Everything was prelude." He cupped her face in his big hands, and she could feel the calluses from his sword. "We both knew we'd finish what we started in the parking lot. For the first time in my life, I *wanted* to create a summoning pact."

She exhaled a breath that sounded suspiciously like a sigh.

"I dream about taking you." His attention dipped to her lips again. "If danger wasn't all around and a severed leg giving us mood music, I'd be kissing you right now, kissing you long and slow. I'd do it till you got so wet for me and craved me inside you so bad. . . . You said you don't beg, but I could *make* you."

The irresistible charge between them dwarfed even the lightning. She angled her chin up. The tip of her tongue decided to daub her bottom lip.

His pupils enlarged as he clocked her mouth. "Fuck, Red, you love to tease me. You play with me."

"*I* play with *you*?"

"You look down on demons. You want a warlock for your man."

"I just want someone who'll be true to me. I don't care what species he is!"

"Yeah?" he asked, his tone saying, *Really?*

"Yeah," she answered, her tone saying, *Duh!* "I can't trust my own magic; I can't trust my fellow Loreans until I find out who cursed me. But I have to be able to trust my partner."

All the ire seemed to drain from him. "No wonder you wouldn't give me the time of night after our date."

"You have to admit the situation looked bad," she said. "And you do have a certain reputation. But now I'm glad we've gotten everything out in the open."

Had his eyes darted?

"Rök?"

"C'mere." He reached for her. "You've picked up a spiderweb." He teased it out of her hair until her lids went heavy, her own irritation melting away.

Though she'd steeled herself against his charisma and effortless charm, this tenderness might prove her undoing.

"I need to focus on keeping you safe." He brushed his knuckles along her jawline. "But when I've delivered you from this place, I'm going to make love to you."

His confidence shouldn't be *that* sexy. "You sound sure of yourself."

"Done deal." His gaze gleamed with anticipation.

Maybe that was exactly what needed to happen. She could enjoy him, getting him out of her system. She wouldn't become a swimbo—because she would never summon him again.

Thud thud thud. That sound broke the moment for Poppy. "More mood music."

He glowered in that direction. "Time to push on, huh?" When she nodded, he took her hand in his, and they continued deeper into the lab.

Was Poppy his fated one? Still doubtful. But Rök was *trying.* And he did care about her.

Expectation filled her, changing her entire outlook. This threatening place didn't bother her. The past didn't bother her. They would find a way out of this lab, break the curse, then enjoy each other.

For just one night.

Buoyed by that knowledge, her steps were lighter, her lips curving on their own.

Reading her thoughts once more, he said, "Everything is prelude again, isn't it?"

They'd reached the curtain, prompting her to remind him, "If we survive."

"The motivation of all motivations." He drew the cloth back, revealing steps to a platform. Chucking her under the chin, he started up.

As they climbed, she murmured, "We're in deep."

"Heard it's the only way to swim," he murmured back. "Just stay frosty."

"Ah-firmative."

Atop the platform stood what looked like an old transformer, with voltage meters and levers. Positioned beside it was a stainless steel table. Metal restraints jutted from it like ribs, but they'd been wrenched open.

Rök tested one of the restraints. "No mean feat to break these. That wizard must've thought *Frankenstein* was a how-to manual—and he actually brought something to life, something strong. How'd he do it? Electricity and magic?"

She nodded. "You'd be amazed at what those two elements can do. Talk about a haunted house with a history."

"Then where's the subject? Was that its blood on the door?" The unspoken question: *Is it inside with us?*

"It can't still be alive, right? It's been locked in here for potentially decades. There's no food. Even the spiders and rats all died out."

"None of this is in my wheelhouse."

She and Rök edged past the gurney. Behind it sprawled a decapitated corpse in a bloodstained lab coat. The severed head lay nearby. White hair covered the scalp, the gnarled face frozen in a macabre scream.

Poppy said, "Meet the castle's owner."

"And more." Rök pointed to a long, lumpen form not far away on the platform. "That was the subject."

An emaciated body lay facing away from them, clad only in tattered pants. Its bare back revealed crisscrosses of staples across its discolored skin. Had the wizard created it out of . . . male Loreans?

Rök whistled low. "Looks like a revenant went through a blender. So this wretch killed its creator, then died? At least it didn't have to tangle with a mob of torch-bearing villagers."

"They would've come in the shitty sequel."

When Rök started toward it, Poppy said, "What are you doing?"

"I can't *not* see it." He seemed entranced, smoke rising from his skin.

"Take it from me: you won't be able to unsee it either."

Rök continued forward, caught in the horror-flick tractor beam. . . .

ELEVEN

Curiosity goading him, Rök approached the body, taking in the stapled skin and wasted muscles. Were those metal bolts on the wretch's neck, like a car battery? "You sure this one isn't yours?"

"My Frankenstein's monster is more creature-feature, all forehead, with green skin like my witches. This one looks somewhat human." She sounded unfazed by their gruesome find, but after the visitors, this must be nothing. "Why hasn't it decomposed more?"

"No idea." Rök stepped closer, had to see its face. He muttered a curse. It was a death mask of anguish: brows drawn, cheeks sunken, teeth clenched. What had this creature gone through? Was its first memory one of electrocution?

Lightning struck the rod yet again, and wires pulsed. A current leapt from a coil to fork out like roots toward the creature. Those neck bolts sparked, and the body convulsed, its spine bowing.

Rök stumbled back. "Holy fuck, it's alive!"

"It's alive?" Poppy asked from behind him.

"It's alive! ALIVE!" Rök went for his sword.

She reached around to snatch his hand. "No conductors!"

With a nod, he yanked Poppy into his arms and leapt to the floor. They watched in disbelief as the creature rolled from the sparking platform onto the ground.

The thrashing ebbed. With the current disrupted, the body stilled. No breaths moved its chest. No heartbeats sounded. Only a residual spark or two crackled around those bolts.

"Or *not* alive." Rök glanced back at that leg in the tank. "The body was jolted." Even so, he squired Poppy away, putting distance between them and the wretch. "That . . . got my attention."

She allowed him to guide her, nonchalant about what they'd just witnessed. "You really are scared of things that come back to life. You screamed like a child."

"Thanks for the memo, Red."

Imitating him, she cried, "It's *alive*! ALIVE!"

"You done?"

"Never!" Growing serious, she said, "I do feel sorry for what it went through. Can you imagine what a true resurrection must feel like?"

Rök *could*. That was the problem. . . .

In the last unexplored section of the lab, they came across the wizard's drafting desk. Its surface held ghastly sketches of a cobbled-together man, like an architect's plans.

A leather-bound journal to the side caught their attention. Rök gazed on as she brushed dust from the cover and flipped through. Blood smeared most of the pages, obscuring the writings, but a raven's feather marked one semi legible entry. It had a date from the last century and a heading.

"*The Ending of Everything*," Rök read. "What does that mean?" And why did it give him chills?

"I remember that date. It was four Halloween full moons

ago. That must have been when his family died." Poppy glanced up at Rök. "Everyone believes the castle opens because the veil between worlds is thinnest on this date. But what if it opens because it's an anniversary of significance?"

They read further: *Four calls of my raven always beckoned them inside. Four calls of the raven came and went, but my family never returned from their nightly play among the tombstones.*

Rök tapped the page. "The castle door opened for us at sunset like it used to, to let his family out to play. In the morning, to the sound of a raven's call, it will open again to call them home to their beds." Not much was random in the Lore. "Only they're never coming back."

"So what happened? Did a rival wizard strike? Or maybe vampires descended on them." She hastily flipped the page.

As I tracked them with my raven, the wizard wrote, *hope dwindled. In the forest, I found carnage. . . .* Blood coated the next few paragraphs. Then: *Gateway nearby to a realm of all undead immortals?*

Between crimson smudges, Rök made out a word or part of one: *mort* or *mord*. "Why would he write about an undead realm in this entry? Do you think . . . ?"

Poppy's eyes widened, and she nodded. "Something about that portrait on the landing struck me. The wife wore an armband. Rök, one of the three ghouls in the cemetery had that same armband! The mother and her two children have been here all this time. They were transformed into ghouls. The undead."

"Of all the fates." Rök stifled a shudder. "I'd much rather be moldering in the ground." Understatement.

"The wizard did experiment to resurrect his family—not from death, but from *undeath.*"

She and Rök fell silent, both lost in thought.

That *Ending of Everything* heading continued to resonate

with him. He felt sympathy for the wizard. If Rök had lost Poppy and their children to ghouls, he feared he would have done far, far worse than experimenting on subjects.

Poppy finally spoke. "When I picture those three forever wandering this property, I pity them." She held Rök's gaze. "But I also feel foreboding." The witch's confidence from the start of the night had vanished.

"Hey, we're going to be fine," he assured her, though her stark expression spooked him a touch. "No way three ghouls can get the best of immortals like us. You aren't a seeress, are you?"

"No, my sister Clove is the budding oracle in our family. But sometimes I feel like I can borrow my sisters' powers. I'll make a shot only a warrioress like Lea could make, or I'll know what cards someone is holding, like Clove always does. And right now I've got a bad feeling about those ghouls."

To distract her, he said, "Why don't you keep that journal? It might have some interesting history. At the very least, it'll net you all kinds of forum cachet."

She stowed the journal in her bag. "We've combed this lab. There's no battery and no way out. I have to use my portal."

"I'm against it in principle. If something happens to me, I need to know you have at least one more at bat."

"We don't have a choice." She collected the pouch. "Unfortunately, I don't know where we'll end up. I'm too turned around to aim inside this castle, can't plot a course for the foyer."

What if her portal took them to another locked room? They could still be trapped within a trap.

She bit her lip. "Maybe I could *try* to get us outside?"

Outside. Away from this place! A part of him clamored for freedom.

But . . . "You told me those visitors won't quit until you're dead. Which means we have to break your curse. Tonight. Witch, I'm all in." To deliver her from the greater, looming threat, he just had to protect his mate against more unkillable visitors, find a cursebreaker to rid her of them, then get her out of here.

She gazed up at him, her green eyes filled with an emotion he barely dared to name. Or claim—

GROOOOOAAN.

Rök and Poppy froze.

"Holy shit," she whispered, "it really *is* alive."

TWELVE

Poppy's gaze combed the shadows. In the flickers of lightning, the creature crawled toward them with lurching movements, electricity sparking along his stapled wounds.

She could all but *feel* how much he must have suffered. "Rök, what are we going to do with him?"

"Do? Look at its eyes."

She peered into the gloom. *Whoa.* Her empathy faded. The creature's black eyes burned with raw malice. That wasn't a man—not a *he*—but wrath embodied.

It opened its mouth wide, clawed hands reaching for them. *My gods, it wants us dead.*

"Behind me, witch. I've got this."

"Let's just get out of here." She rubbed her thumb over her final pouch, and magic seeped into her. Rök's selflessness—*I'm all in*—called to her own. Despite her desperation for the cursebreaker, she couldn't risk him any longer. She aimed her portal for home. . . .

Magic said, *Hard no.*

Which meant there was no mystical way out of this place.

She probed the castle for any kind of power source—maybe they could in fact shut down the battery—and tried to direct her portal there. The air shifted before her, opening a threshold to a dimly lit room. Looked like an attic.

GROOOOOAAN. The creature lumbered to stand. Must be seven feet tall!

"It's walking!" Rök said in horrified wonder. "You seeing this?"

Poppy yanked on his hand. "Come on!"

With a last fascinated look, Rök followed her across the threshold.

She muttered the incantation to seal it. As the portal began to close, the creature roared with fury and limped faster.

Rök turned back and raised his sword to block. "Think again, fiend."

Uncaring, it clumsily dove, black eyes wide. . . .

The portal blipped closed right in the creature's face. A bellow of rage reverberated across the castle.

Once the sound tapered away, Poppy exhaled a breath and scanned their surroundings. A tepid lantern lit a pitch-ceilinged room that must stretch over most of the castle. Scattered toys, clothes, and broken bits of furniture from a bygone era smelled of cedar and dust. Dolls lined a shelf.

Rök tensed at the sight of them. "Bloody hell! Those yours?" He leapt forward and swung his sword, slicing through the dolls.

In a dry tone, she said, "Innocent toys were harmed in the filming of this scene."

"Smart-ass. You'll have to excuse my caution." His attention turned to a pair of dormer windows, buffeted by the wind in the stormy night. He attempted to open them, but they were sealed. "Why did your portal take us here?"

"I tried to aim it toward a power source, but I don't sense the battery."

He crossed to a nearby door, which opened easily. "It's a stairwell. We can walk right out."

A piece of luck. "How about a short rest then?" They hadn't slowed for an instant, and fueling her visitors took a toll. This curse was like a millstone she could never lose, one that grew heavier each Halloween.

"Sounds good. Just let me clear the area."

As he scouted for bogeys, she processed what they'd seen. "Do you think the creature will find a way out of that lab?"

"Depends on how clever it is. And how clever that wizard was." Rök investigated the attic, checking wardrobes and chests. He relaxed by degrees, his ease calling to her own.

Sitting on a large pile of quilts, she retrieved her thermos. "You want some pumpkin spice tea?"

"Sure." He sheathed his sword and joined her.

Passing the thermos back and forth reminded her of tasting wines at their dinner, sharing glasses with him. For the first time, she was able to recall that night in a different light. She hadn't imagined their affinity—Rök truly had enjoyed bantering with her and getting to know her better.

One aspect she hadn't noted was his reaction to the summoning. His brows had drawn together as he'd uttered her name, and his grip on her hand had tightened.

Being summoned wasn't a power trip for Rök; it was a burden.

Had her anger over his disappearance clouded her memory? She set down the thermos, remembering other details about their interactions.

Over the last few years, she'd had some lucky breaks on jobs, and each had been marked by the *scent of smoke*. Her lips parted. At varying times, the demon had traced and helped her, doing everything from removing an enemy to diverting a rockslide that had narrowly missed her.

She even recalled throwing precious magic his way to assist him as well. As if she couldn't stand to see him hurt.

She glanced around at all the forgotten knickknacks. Attics often preserved the past. Was a wizard's attic making Poppy remember hers more clearly?

"Do you sense the prize?" Rök studied her expression.

"Magic is thick here, but it feels like . . . memories. Like if the castle was a person, this would be a storehouse of memories."

"Never a dull moment with you."

Had he reached his limit of mystical bullshit? She had, and she was a witch! "You thought I could portal us out of here—to safety and cocktails—and you told me not to."

"Because we've still got work to do."

We. "For the record, I did try to get us out. This situation isn't fair to you."

"Red, no. You came here for a cursebreaker, and we'll find it."

"What about the visitors? I still sense that they're going to return in a big way. Going head-to-head against them isn't logical."

"I can't believe I'm about to say this, but if they show, we run. We evade them while we search. But you will be free of this curse." He curled a finger under her chin. As he stared down at her, his irises grew gray with feeling, displaying that Rök-type tenderness. "The visitors are a danger to you, so we have to defeat them. Woman, understand me: I'll take on hell for you."

Oh, Rök. Earlier when she'd realized that the visitors would kill everyone she loved, she'd also feared that this ladies' man might be *among that number.*

He is. She did feel love for him.

Involuntary.

Foolish.

Love.

"Poppy, you're mission critical to me." Something a merc couldn't live without.

Her breath caught. Emotion demanded an outlet. *Screw it. Screw self-respect.* She grabbed his nape and dragged him down to meet her lips.

He groaned with readiness, cupping her face with those big, callused palms. He slanted his head to take her mouth deeper, seeming to breathe in her moan when their tongues met.

She sensed need seething inside him, but he kissed her languidly, stoking her desire as if they had all the time in the worlds. He built the tension like a controlled burn—demon-hot and mind-numbing in its intensity.

Yet then he drew back. "There's still danger." His voice had grown rumbly. His scent was embers.

Dazed with lust, she stared at his lips. "Danger? Oh. Well, you've convinced me we can handle it. Let's release a little steam. We'll be able to concentrate on the mission better." She grabbed him once more. Against his mouth, she said, "I have to experience you. Just once."

He drew back his head again. "*Once?*"

"You don't have to worry about my summoning you. I'm stronger than that." She was. She *was*.

"Listen, I need to tell you something."

"No, you don't." How could a player's confessions make her *more* likely to sleep with him? *I'm 100 percent a sure thing.* "I need you to do things with your mouth, and I don't mean talking."

He looked intrigued by that, distracted, but then his expression hardened. "You should hear what I have to say." His tone was reasonable, even as his horns swelled.

She wanted to pet them and see if the rumors were true. Would he truly lose his mind if she gripped them? The prospect excited her even more! She went up on her knees to undress. "Quick. We don't have forever." As she removed her clothes, she might've been shy about her body or wished parts were different, but after seeing trends come and go for a hundred years, she gave sweet fuck-all about the body image du jour.

When she knelt before him in only her black underwear and demi bra, he appeared staggered. "Ah, Red." Her nipples budding against tight silk had him riveted. "I can't resist even your opening volley." His talking *merc* was just icing on the cake.

"I'm waiting." She unclasped her bra, loving his brows-drawn look as her breasts swayed.

"Dark gods below." Rök shook his head hard, as if he stared at a mirage.

With a proud grin, she squared her shoulders—

"Fuck it, let's deploy!" He bounded to his feet and tore off his bloodstained shirt to reveal brawny muscles and healing knife wounds.

Wounds earned from defending her. Poppy's heart went *pang*, even as her body went *want*.

He toed off his boots, tripping before righting himself.

"You have done this before, right?"

"Once or twice." He shoved down his pants, kicking them away.

His erection bobbed before her spellbound eyes. *It figures he'd be magnificent there too.* And he knew it, was sure to give her time to ogle him.

Once she could tear her gaze away, she raked it over the rest of his body from his horns down to his toes and back up. The sight of his ripped physique primed her as never before.

But her attention couldn't stray for long from his cock. Each inch of it invited adoration. As she licked her lips for that distended flesh, she imagined tasting the broad head . . . tonguing down the meaty shaft . . . to those weighty balls.

Her appetite for his dick turned carnal, her witchly greed finding a new target. *Want to nip, tease, and tug. Wrench groans from his lungs. Make him* wish *I'd summon him . . .*

Though she could have stared for hours, he half-tackled her atop the quilts. She'd expected practiced smoothness from such a player, but this barely harnessed aggression was *doing it for her.*

When she wriggled from her panties, he swallowed hard. "I might have done this once or twice, but I can't quite remember a single time before you."

Awww. Making her voice a purr, she said, "You heard something tasty was here tonight and you wanted to jump all over it? There is. You may."

Amusement lit his sinful expression as he moved between her thighs. "Oh, *may* I? If you think that's how the dynamic between us will play out . . ." He trailed off when she let her knees fall wide. The demon's eyes grew glazed as he turned a one-syllable word into three: *"Fuh huh kuhk."*

THIRTEEN

Mind blank.
Mind.

Blank.

Too beautiful. Rök felt like he'd been awestruck at the sight of the divine.

Damp curls framed glistening, pink flesh. His tongue flicked in his mouth for a taste. Her little clit was taut and plump, must ache. He understood—his cock, horns, and fangs pained him as never before.

Take it slow warred with *DEVOUR HER*.

Her intoxicating scent made him as high as opium. When she undulated her hips, the entry to her sex beckoned, and demonic urges racked him. He burned to mount her, mate her, thrusting his cock inside her sheath until they both reached oblivion.

Mine. He ran his swollen horns along one of her pale thighs. The other. He rubbed across her belly and breasts. *All mine.*

She sat up on her elbows and gasped, "Demon!"

"Problem with that?" If Wiccans didn't have mates, how to get her to sign on for more? Only one time frame would do: *forever.*

In answer, she parted her thighs even more, like an offering. The altar of everything.

On his knees before her, breaths ragged, he gripped her breasts with his claw-tipped fingers.

She arched to his touch, pressing her flesh into his palms—yet more offering.

Fondling her, he lowered his head. He dragged his tongue over one nipple, then circled the damp tip.

Her gasp was a lash at his back. How would he last? Urgency gripped him, but he'd give her no hint of it.

He drew the pouting point between his lips, wetting it and flicking. Then he turned to her other nipple. To the music of her breathless moans, he suckled.

"Rök . . . *more!*"

Just like his fantasies. They shared a look over her breast.

Releasing his suck, he kissed down her body to nuzzle the fire-red hair on her mons, luxuriating in her scent and the delights he'd soon enjoy. "I want you so fucking much, Poppy," he rasped. "*All* of you." But first they needed to burn away the worst of their lust. Before he claimed her, he'd tell her the truth. *You're my mate.* She would listen once they'd found some relief.

"*Yes.* I want you too, Rök."

It would happen this very night. Sheer joy swept him up, and he smiled against her curls.

Until she added, "I meant what I said—you don't have to worry about me summoning you. I won't act on any pact we make."

He leaned up with a scowl. "Because I'm not romantic partner material?" Just as he'd been warned—she was his, but he wasn't hers. The idea filled him with aggression. "Then I'm going to eat you like you're my last godsdamned meal, make you come so hard, you'll *have* to summon me every night for the rest of your life."

He fitted his splayed fingers around the globes of her ass and pressed his mouth to her sex. The luscious, slick bliss that greeted him ripped a growl from his chest.

She moaned, "Kiss me, demon. Kiss . . ."

Her taste was a beacon, signaling his demonic instincts. *Lave. Drink. Feast.* His pointed tongue made contact with her clitoris.

"Ahhhh!" she cried, already on the verge.

He lightly licked her bud. *Flick flick.* Not enough to bring her off; just enough to madden her. Nuzzling and licking, he demanded, "You like your demon's tongue?" *Flick flick.* He eased lower to spear her opening for more of her tantalizing nectar.

"Ah, Hecate, yes!" She wetted his lips with her own.

As he kissed, his hips rocked, grinding his length against the quilts. He'd never been so hard. So weirdly emotional. After more than a millennium of waiting, he was pleasuring his mate! *At long last . . .*

Even if she never wanted him to again.

Her cries grew needier. "Finish me!"

His cock threatened to go off spontaneously; still, he bit out, "Ah-ah. Maybe I should torment you to distraction." He worked a finger inside her wetness, leisurely fucking her with it as he tongued her clit. "I could *make* you want more."

"It's already torment. Demon, I ache so bad!" Her head thrashed. "This is even better than I imagined."

He jolted. "Did you fantasize about me, witch?"

Lost, she nodded.

He lashed her bud harder, praising her. "Did you finger this sweet pussy to thoughts of me?"

Her lids fluttered. "I did. I do. A lot."

A savage thrill pierced him like a surprise sword strike.

"More demon! I need *more.*"

"And I'll give it to you once you promise me—"

She seized his horns and yanked him closer.

"POPPY?"

Bucking to his mouth, she took her climax. Took his sanity. His control.

Her scream of rapture echoed as she writhed and writhed to wring her pleasure.

He tasted his mate's orgasm, couldn't lick it fast enough. As her core clenched his finger, frenzy hit. A haze covered his vision—any thoughts of teasing vanished.

The torment is all mine.

Poppy released his horns as she came down from the most realms-shattering orgasm she'd ever had. She'd known getting off with Rök would boggle her brain.

"You're not done." His voice was unrecognizable—*demonic.* Smoke rose from the tips of his flared horns as he kept kissing her, doing wicked things with that talented tongue. "I'll drink you down. We're not done!"

To her surprise . . . he was right. Tension gathered anew. She would definitely need another night of this. Just one summoning, but then never again!

Craving his taste, she gestured for his cock. "Want to kiss you too. Sixty-nine?"

His hips seemed to surge out of his control. Rising above her with feverish gray eyes and swollen muscles, he growled a sound, something like: *"Guh-yeah!"* He maneuvered until they lay side by side, ready to partake.

She took him in hand, marveling at his girth. As Rök set back in with his heated kiss, she could tell he was holding his breath, awaiting hers.

When she leaned in and darted her tongue around the tip,

his puff of exhalation briefly cooled her sex. He'd threatened her with torment? She'd show him torment.

She bestowed kitten licks from his heavy balls . . . following that raised vein upward . . . to the slit along his flared crown . . . and back down.

Flitting her tongue. Fluttering it. Worshipping.

He growled against her. A nip on her thigh told her the demon was done with teasing.

Taking pity on him, she sucked him between her lips as she stroked the thick base of his shaft, finding a loving rhythm. But it wasn't enough. As he sent her rocketing toward the precipice again, she grew hungrier. Hungrier. Until she was bobbing on his length, cheeks hollowed with suction.

He groaned desperately, and his cock pulsed in her mouth. She savored the feel of his mighty flesh and his . . . essence?

She slowed. Had she detected a hint of salt? Precum? Another pulsation; another hint of seed.

Wait . . . A male demon couldn't produce semen unless he was with his mate.

She broke away, gasping with realization. "Oh my gods, it all makes sense!"

He grunted something incomprehensible against her. Then he commanded, "Keep. Sucking. Witch. Your mouth . . . gods . . . you're slaying me!"

His reaction almost seduced her, but this was too important.

"I know why Desh broke his promise of confidentiality. I know what leverage you used with him!"

Rök rolled onto his back, looking like he was having trouble coming back down to this realm. His engorged penis twitched. When she could peel her gaze from it, she found his fists clenched and his eyes narrowed. "Hottest blow job of my life, and you're thinking about Desh? *Desh??* Going to kill that godsforsaken pirate."

She scrambled away, finding her underwear and bra. "You told him I'm your mate! That's why he brought you here and ditched me into your care. A demon would bend the rules for a fellow demon whose mate might be in jeopardy." She dragged clothes on. "You asshole! You knew I was yours, and you didn't tell me?"

As if she hadn't spoken, he yanked up his pants and bounded to his feet. "Desh, really?" Zipping his jeans over his dick without a care, Rök paced. She'd never seen him this unmoored. Almost to himself, he said, "Bad enough when you were with that warlock. I couldn't off him for that, right? I mean, I *could.* Went to his house to do it. But hell, if you found out a demon had hunted your suitors, it would be over before it started."

"It? Are you talking about matehood?" Her wild accusations were, like, *true*? "You'd murder a rival? You Neanderthalian demon!"

"Demons were never Neanderthals," he said absently, still pacing. "Why were you thinking about Desh when your lips were around me? When you were breaking my will with your tongue?" He slowed to face her, looking confounded. "Why are we not coming together right now?"

"Because I tasted you, and then some puzzle pieces fell into place. But I can't be yours."

His bulging jaw muscles said it all.

Oh, Hecate. "You can't be sure until you claim a female. You're supposed to attempt them, right? What's that saying? In the throes you know!"

"Maybe for some. But I knew the night of our date."

Poppy was his fated female? The only one he'd get—*ever*? Though she'd dreamed about this exact scenario, now, the pressure felt too intense. "You . . . didn't say anything."

"I was about to, but you told me to do other things with my mouth, remember?"

"You couldn't have revealed this nugget at any time over the past two years?" The words hung in the air as more memories bloomed. Suddenly she realized what Rök had mouthed to her across a crowd of rowdy Loreans. *You—are—mine.* "The bonfire . . ."

"Yeah, I told you that night. And how'd you react? You portaled away like it was the last evac out of a hot zone! I tried to convince myself you didn't understand me."

"I didn't!"

"Would it have made a difference? You were dating that warlock. Gods below, I wanted that prick dead. Only the thought of hurting you kept me from taking his head." Rök's eyes blazed, his fangs sharpening. "I'll say this again—I can't help what I am. And I am bloody *done* denying what I feel for you." As smoke rose from his tanned chest, he stalked closer to her, looking dangerous and so sexy her mind nearly blanked. "I am done with pain, done with craving! The demon in me will have his due. *You.*"

On the tip of her tongue: *Take that energy you've got going on and fucking ravish me.*

But she had too many questions, and she was furious to only now be learning about—

Rattle rattle rattle . . . sliiice.

The sound came from a far corner of the attic. Movement appeared deep in the shadows. "The skeletons are coming!"

Rök grated a curse in Demonish and stomped into his boots. "Their timing is infernal."

She yanked on her jacket and bag, probing her curse. "It's not just them. I feel them *all* stirring." She and Rök would have to deal with this shocking revelation later. "It's bad. Worse than ever before." To punctuate her statement, the angry shriek of a horse sounded from somewhere in the castle.

Rök donned his shirt. "That what I think it is?"

Nod. "The Headless Horseman."

FOURTEEN

W̶e don't have any way to dispose of the skeletons here."
Rök belted his sword, not that it'd inflict lasting damage
against these foes. "We've got to run. Rain check?"

She glared. "Undecided."

Fantastic. He'd said too much. He'd let his thwarted need
and the memory of all those crazed nights away from her goad
his temper.

When skeletons emerged from the shadows, scythes raised,
he said, "Witch, we are *leaving*," and grabbed her hand. With
another glare, she allowed it. They hurried to the exit, and he
opened the door.

A flood of black flew at them.

"Down!" He snagged her and hit the ground, shielding her
from a swarm of vampire bats. "Those yours?"

Above their screeches, she said, "Mine. It wouldn't be—"

"Halloween without them. Yeah, yeah."

The flying rats blotted the air, wings flapping, bodies
colliding. But once the skeletons drew closer, the swarm
vanished as if it'd never been.

Pulling her to her feet, Rök led her through the doorway and down the creaking steps. "Let's lose them—" Wood crumbled beneath his boots.

"Rök!" She snatched him back, and they watched the rotted step fall. All the ones below it looked unstable. Rusted nails squeaked under their weight.

Rattle rattle rattle . . . sliiice.

"We've still got to head down. Stay close to the side." Hastening as much as they dared, they made it down one rickety flight.

Above them skeletons plowed into each other and plummeted through that missing step. Bones rained over Rök and Poppy. A skull bounced atop her shoulder, still snapping at her!

Rök swatted it away, then caught a scythe right over Poppy's head. He flung it back at their pursuers as he led her down . . . down . . . down . . . a never-ending stairway. "Hate this place!"

When they'd gained a small lead, Poppy asked, "How did you stay away from me?"

He glanced back at her as they charged on. "We doing this now?"

"Might not get another chance. Let me guess, you buried yourself in other women to forget about your mate. Racking up the swimbos!" Her eyes glowed from more than a power outlay.

In any other circumstance, he would've relished her jealousy. "I haven't been with anyone since before our date."

"Celibate for years? Tell me another whopper, smoke and mirrors."

"I let every summoner know I thought I was mated, which was as awkward as you can imagine."

In a stunned tone, she said, "I believe you. Should I be astounded or insulted that you're the only Lorean who *avoided* his fated female?"

"You didn't want to be near me! Not exactly encouraging."

"Other males get crazed, and you just held back. I hear about these guys all the time."

"I hear about them too! But I know you. You wouldn't have put up with that shit for a nanosecond. Am I a crazed smoke demon who's obsessed with you? Yeah. Did you need to see that? No."

"You're . . . obsessed with me?"

With weary acceptance, he said, "The definition of it."

"Oh, gods, that's why you keep booking deadly jobs. For a distraction! How long would you have waited?"

"You were dating that warlock, remember. I thought you needed to be with him to unlock your powers. No male wants to be the reason his mate doesn't thrive. I wanted what's best *for you.* Even if that's *not me.*"

Her expression softened at his words, yet then her eyes widened. "Lea got to you!"

He raised his chin a notch. Unwilling concession.

"When?" Poppy demanded, planning to throttle her oldest sister.

"Lea's my sister by fate. I don't want to throw her under the bus."

"She had no right to interfere with my life!"

"Doesn't she have a point though? One of the reasons I stayed away is because I thought you wanted a relationship like your parents have."

The storybook Wiccans. "I tried it their way."

And while Poppy had been burying her feelings for this

demon, Rök had been risking his life on jobs. Suffering. Trying to do right by her.

Rattle rattle rattle . . . sliiice. Another contingent of skeletons charged *up* the steps to meet them. He kicked the closest one in the sternum, sending it stumbling back to knock the others down. "Come on!" He pulled Poppy into his arms to wend around bones, dodging the chomping skulls around his boots.

When he'd cleared the worst, he kept her in his arms—and she kept questioning him. "Why come here tonight?" Despite the danger, she wanted answers. "What changed?"

"Your breaking up with the warlock was like a crack in the dam for me. I realized that where you're concerned, maybe I've grown greedy and selfish and as far from decent as a demon can be. If I'm to be denied, it should be because *you* say no. Not because I do."

His confessions would've made her heart stutter if their lives hadn't been on the line. Feelings had blindsided this poor, bewildered male.

"A split second after I realized I wasn't strong enough to stay away from you any longer, I heard your sister threatening Desh."

What was that saying? *Sometimes fate doesn't bother being subtle.* Poppy tightened her arms around Rök's neck.

A different kind of nightmare, a goblin with a pumpkin head and green-stalk body, lumbered up the stairs carrying an ax.

"Jack O'Lantern." Poppy itched for a pouch to wipe that weird leer off its gourd. "Watch out for its—"

Stalk tentacles whipped out, coiling around Rök's legs.

"—stalk tentacles."

Rök dodged an ax blow, then swung his sword to sever the stalks. They grew back in a flash, lashing out at him.

With Poppy tucked against him, Rök evaded another ax strike, then slashed the pumpkin head. Two orange halves thudded to the stairs, seeds oozing out like brain matter. The misshapen body and stalks collapsed and withered. Rök kicked free and sidled past the remains, sheathing his sword.

Poppy, dogged, kept at him. "How could I have a say in this—denying you or not—if I don't know my options?"

Cradling her in his arms, he vaulted over a series of missing steps. "I'm laying everything on the line now. I want *you*. For all time." Never slowing their flight, he held her gaze. "Is my entire life's objective—the most important mission of them all—doomed to failure?"

He ran down the steps. They stared at each other. He ran.

"Well, Red? Don't leave me hanging."

Her chin tilted up a notch.

"Hell, yeah!" he exclaimed. "Let's survive this night and then sort our shit out."

"It's a lot of shit to sort. You left me hanging for years! What were you thinking? When did acting noble ever work out for mercs like us?"

He'd given her time. The one thing she hadn't wanted from him. Now she felt *out of time*.

"Noble won't happen again, love."

A landing appeared! When they reached the floor, she wanted to kiss it. Three doors awaited them. "Which one?"

Rök chose the closest. "This looks good."

From the other side, a whispery sound slithered into her hearing. *Kill kill kill puh puh puh.* "Wait!"

Rök had already opened the door, coming face-to-face with the gigantic camp slasher. Behind his mask, a murderous hunger burned in his eyes. The machete he carried glinted in the dim hall light.

Rök dropped Poppy and readied his sword. When the machete flashed out, Rök blocked the blade with his own, then doubled back for a swift hit. His sword struck true; the slasher's hand and machete flew into the air. Never slowing his momentum, Rök targeted the madman's legs, severing them above the knee with one gory sweep.

Blood spurted as the slasher collapsed to the floor.

"Come on, Poppy, keep moving!"

As Rök urged her away, she glanced back at the writhing slasher. He grunted manically, a thrill killer denied his prey.

How could that thing be connected to her? Why *this* curse? Why nightmares? Was it because she'd always liked spooky stories?

With more caution, Rök opened the next door. No bogeys awaited them. He and Poppy dashed from the castle, only to be greeted by a thorny wall of hedges in an outdoor courtyard.

"Outside, finally!" Rök tried to trace them, but they didn't budge. "We're still within the castle's boundary?"

She glanced up at the rain pattering against an invisible barrier. "Looks like."

Rök jerked his chin at the sole opening in the dense hedge. "That's a labyrinth."

"With a twist." Poppy recognized that thorny species. Her sister Sage joked that its Latin name should be *Sittingus Duckingus*. "Those briars carry a paralytic agent." Though the plants appeared to have been dead for some time, their thorns would still be toxic.

"I can vault over them."

"One scratch for either of us, and we'd be helpless for hours." Sitting ducks. "Let's head back. The landing had a third door." They'd just turned in that direction when children's laughter sounded, accompanied by the tip-tap of little shoes.

"Shit! Annelise and her friends are back."

HISSSSSS. StStSt. HISSSSSS.

"Aliens too," Rök said. "Looks like we're heading into the maze."

"Halloween labyrinths never work out well for the maze-goer."

"Open to ideas."

"Okay, we'll go. But not one scratch. Remember, I don't have any pouches left to help us."

"Got it." Gravel crunched beneath their boots as they started in. Overgrown limbs seemed to stretch toward them, thorny fingers grasping. He hacked at them with his sword.

As they hastened down the prickly corridor, creaking metal sounded from behind them. Rök said, "Just heard something not so good."

"Haunted suits of armor. Watch for maces. I'm feeling some ghosts too."

Floating apparitions shook the limbs and moaned, *"Whooo whooo . . ."*

"When you said a tsunami of shit, you meant it."

Yes. Because nightmares were infinite.

She and Rök had just turned the first corner when a pair of maces burst through the hedge from different directions, both heading for her face.

He blocked one with his sword and caught the other in his fist, gritting his teeth against the spikes. As he tossed those weapons away, more maces swung toward them. "Keep moving!" He and Poppy sprinted forward.

Dodging strikes, they turned left. They curved right. Ducking and sliding.

Whenever they came to a fork, maces would spur them in a particular direction. Between breaths, she said, "They're steering us."

"Getting that feeling."

High above them, an apparition shook the limbs, sending thorns flying. Rök yanked Poppy to his chest just in time to shield her.

Once the downpour ended, she said, "Tell me you didn't get barbed."

"I don't think so." He tugged her along, and they rounded another corner. "I see the exit!" The corridor ended about two hundred feet away. Beyond the maze, a pair of double doors marked another castle entry point. "We're close." Yet then Rök stumbled.

It'd been cute when he'd stripped. Not so much now. "You tripped over your feet running from bogeys."

"Yeah, I know."

"Like a blonde in the woods."

"Yeah, I know!"

"I'll never let you live this down."

"Yeah . . . I *know*." Was he slurring?

Poppy dropped back to scan the demon. "Oh, Hecate!" Thorns dotted his back.

He slowed. "What?"

"You don't feel anything?" The toxin was already working. "We've got to get these out."

He turned to her. His pupils were enlarged, his skin clammy.

"I need your sword." When he handed it over, she used the edge to scrape the briars free.

He scowled at the growing pile of barbs atop the gravel. "How long before those hit me?"

"In less than twenty minutes, you won't be able to move."

Most people would have panicked; he looked resolved. "Then I've got that long to get you out of here. You're going to be . . . the final girl . . . if it kills me." He reclaimed his sword.

"By definition that means you *do* get killed."

"You know . . . what I mean."

He was about to lose the use of his body, and she couldn't protect him. She had no pouches. No abilities. No ally to save the day.

Another mace struck, missing them by inches. "Rök, they *are* steering us."

"To where?"

A horse's shriek sounded from the direction of those doors.

Eyes looking black from the toxin, Rök said, "If they want us to go to there . . . then we head back. Do not go through those doors!"

She nodded, and they reversed course.

A snarling mass of foes blocked their way. The killer clown and the healed camp slasher had materialized. The fiend with the razor gloves and Jack O'Lantern too. Aliens and gremlins emerged from the hedge walls. Annelise and the other dolls balanced atop thorny limbs.

"We've gotta break through them." Rök swiped his eyes. "Stay right behind me."

"You can't fight them all!"

He chucked her under the chin. "When I said I'd take on hell for you . . . I meant it." He faced the visitors with his horns sharpened and fangs bared. Raising his sword, he roared until the hedges trembled.

He couldn't trace; he had no smoke. And still he charged. . . .

Sword and weapons clashed. Parries and blocks. Muscles slashed, skin flayed.

He would slice one foe with his sword while mauling another with his claws. Fire and ice.

Poppy held her breath as he fought, kept digging into her satchel from habit. A bystander at her own battle, she could do nothing but silently urge him on and flinch with each hit he sustained.

He'd "killed" most of them at least once. Though he'd dispatched five aliens, seven regrouped. And the toxin seemed to prevent him from accessing his demonic self. Which meant the battle was a losing one.

Then came the coup de grâce, the strike that ended all hope of victory: one wave of a blank-eyed doll's arm.

Poppy's and Rök's bodies left the ground once more.

FIFTEEN

Annelise's telekinesis launched them down the maze to crash through the double doors. They tumbled across a hardwood floor, his loose sword clanging on the wood.

Poppy scrambled to her feet. "Rök!" She rushed toward his motionless form some distance away, struggling to get her bearings.

Gas chandeliers cast a wavering light over an enormous ballroom. Towering windows framed lightning from the storm outside. Between them, grim-faced portraits gazed down at the sheet-draped furniture and statues that lined the perimeter of the room.

"Poppy," Rök muttered. "Can't bloody move."

"I'm coming!" Before she could reach him, visitors appeared and blocked her way. She darted to her right; more appeared. To her left, more visitors.

Within moments, they'd filled the ballroom. Even the earliest manifestations of her curse had shown: vampires, werewolves, and more.

As they closed in on her, Poppy kept Rök in sight. The slasher leaned down to grip one of his arms, the killer clown grabbing his other. When they dragged Rök's limp body upright, his head lolled.

Never had she hungered so for power. The curse that had threatened her sanity would now take her life—and his.

Why hadn't she loved him when she'd had the chance? Why hadn't they talked? She should have chewed him out two years ago! They could have aired their differences.

All that wasted time.

Grury was back. But the fury overwhelmed her grief. She couldn't allow this scourge to win. She couldn't allow them to hurt the demon she loved.

The slasher gripped Rök's hair, snatching his head up. Rök's glowing gaze darted until he found hers. He tried to speak and couldn't. He barely managed to mouth, *Run!* He wasn't worried about himself, only her.

Did he not understand that she'd never leave him behind? She couldn't have even when she'd thought she hated him. Now . . .

Love.

The visitors near him parted, a broad aisle revealing the ultimate nightmare on the far side of the ballroom: the Headless Horseman. His steed reared on its hind legs, front hooves punching the air. When the Horseman spurred his mount and charged, Rök's captors made horrible sounds of excitement, awaiting the killing blow. . . .

"No, no, no!" Her fury morphed to ungovernable rage. A strange heat coursed through her veins. Magic permeated the air.

From me?

Her body began to vibrate. She glanced at her hands. They shook so fast she couldn't make them out. The hardwood floor buckled beneath the force of her quaking body. *What's happening to me?*

The Horseman neared Rök, galloping hooves sounding over the din of the monsters.

All the while, her vibrations intensified, marking some ability she'd never known. Though she'd found no talisman here, magic tolled inside her, the force too great to be contained. Was it enough?

When the Horseman freed his sword with a ringing pitch, the demon briefly closed his eyes. He opened them to stare at her. She saw her feelings mirrored in them.

Love. Yes.

As their gazes met, she instinctively knew what to do in order to end decades of her suffering and to save her demon.

Picturing every villain here dying bloody, she raised her hands, threw back her head, and screamed: *"ENOUGH!"*

From her quaking form, light and magic exploded like a mystical star . . . funneling out . . . out . . . before boomeranging back to her.

Silence.

Then came the sound of a body dropping on the wood floor. Her head dipped, her gaze seeking Rök's.

He'd collapsed, still paralyzed—and all the nightmares . . . had vanished. Not a sound from them, not a hint of them.

She ran to Rök. "Demon!" She dropped to her knees beside his motionless form, cradling his head in her lap.

With difficulty, he said, "Break curse?"

"I . . . maybe?" She couldn't explain it. She'd stopped the visitors, yes. And she didn't think she'd have to tangle with them again tonight. But they weren't *gone*. She didn't feel free.

Had she merely muted the curse? Maybe she'd always possessed that muting ability but had just needed the proper motivation to access it: *saving Rök from a beheading.* "We don't have to worry about them. Whatever I came here to do has been done. The visitors are on hiatus."

"Without a . . . cursebreaker?"

"To be fair, Mariketa never told me to expect one in this castle, just an answer." And yet it'd come with even more questions. Poppy would visit the young witch again and drill down on this new power.

Rök tried to nod, might have bobbed his head.

"Let's get you more comfortable." She spotted a covered divan along a wall and hauled him over. Dragging off the dust cover, she managed to lift him and maneuvered him to a sitting position.

"You . . . did *something*." Curiosity lit his expression.

"I think I might be able to ward off curses or to mute them." Mariketa had also mentioned a prize; she must've meant this ability. But then, who could steal it from Poppy? "We'll figure everything out in time. For now, concentrate on shaking off the toxin."

"I'll be back to normal soon."

Not likely. "Can you drink some tea?"

"Pumpkin spice? Had my fill of pumpkin for the night." He frowned. "Why do you look so pensive? Shouldn't we be celebrating?"

She forced a smile. "Just tired. I had to fuel a lot of visitors." Even as she said the words, her earlier sense of foreboding returned. Thoughts of the missing explorers floated into her consciousness.

"You're the worst liar I've ever met. Tell me what's going on."

Sighing, she admitted, "I sense more danger coming."

He looked increasingly alert, his attention landing on his sword across the ballroom. "Imminent danger?"

"Not imminent. Nothing is on its way, but I get the feeling the other explorers might have met a bad fate and that we might too. It's like I've got all the clues yet can't see the pattern."

He caught her gaze. "You want to know what I see? My mate before me. Together, we can do anything. The two of us as a team will be unstoppable." He reached for her face with both hands, surprising them both.

"That toxin should've lasted hours more!"

"Feeling's returning all over. I'm a mated demon, remember? All my new strength is meant to protect you." He glanced down; blood rushed back to one area especially. "And to pleasure you."

That sight made her melt. "I thought demons only got stronger *after* claiming their mate."

"Ah, I like how your merc mind works. You want me to claim you so I'll be a better asset in our future battles. If I must . . ."

"Don't put words into my mouth."

"Gods, don't remind me of putting things into your mouth." His erection strained in his jeans.

She absently asked, "Are you trying to distract me from my concerns?"

"You're staring at my cock like a vampire eyeing an artery, so I'd say it's working."

"We do have unfinished business." She dragged her gaze away from his crotch. "But your injuries . . ."

"Forgotten." His emphatic tone made her grin. He managed to swing his legs around. "Are you sure the visitors are done?"

She nodded. "For now."

Rök stood, testing his muscles and stretching his limbs. With long, surefooted strides, he retrieved his sword and sheathed it with one try.

As he returned to her with his shoulders back and his blue gaze focused on her face, she regarded him with a new eye. Was that magnificent demon truly . . . hers?

Sitting beside her on the divan, he grew serious as he said,

"I only stayed away from you because I wanted what's best for you."

"And you suffered for that."

He didn't deny it.

"You told me you knew I was yours during our date," she said. "How?"

"I'd sensed something different about you even before then. Your scent got me strung tight, and competing on jobs against you felt wrong. First time in my life I was pulling for a competitor to win. Then I realized that seeing you was the only highlight in my life, the one thing that got me going," he said, making her heart clench and filling her with elation. "During our date, suspicion turned to confidence." He canted his head. "When did you know about me?"

She blinked. "Know?"

"Smart-ass." Lightning flashed, the storm still raging. He glanced around the eerie ballroom then back to her. "I thought we were done for. I really did. And I had so many regrets. I wished I'd been spending the last two years with you. I don't want to waste another minute."

"Me neither." *We might not have as long as we'd hoped.* Time to go out with a bang? "I want more. I need all of you."

"For good?"

She cast him a saucy look. "For *now*. Earn it, demon."

Eyes lively, he said, "Oh, fuck me, witch. I like these challenges."

I know. She leaned forward and nipped his bottom lip.

SIXTEEN

Rök groaned when Poppy released his lip, but he couldn't quite settle in.

With each flare of lightning, the draped statues seemed to creep closer. The faces in the portraits appeared to sneer before shifting back to grim disapproval. "For our first time, I imagined taking you to a nicer place."

She removed her bag and jacket. "Oh, really? You would've screwed me in that restaurant parking lot, and don't you deny it." He had to grin. "Besides, I'm a witch, you're a demon, and it's Halloween. If two mercs like us were ever going to get it on, it *should* be in a place with flickering chandeliers, wandering-eye portraits, and Casper-like dust covers. The setting isn't romantic. But it *fits*."

His mate had a point. "Never dull with you, Poppy. Though shouldn't we be searching for the castle's battery so we can get the hell out?"

"It might not even be here, but gateways to other realms could be. What if we stumble across one? I mean, *something* happened to the previous explorers."

Another good point. Those Loreans had been strong and skilled, yet some circumstance or enemy had bested them.

She checked her watch. "I vote we stay here until closer to moonset, then exit the castle the way we entered."

At least here they had a clear vantage.

"Which gives us some time." She made short work of her boots and jeans. When she peeled off her top, all his protests were forgotten.

This is the vantage I want, he thought as she removed her bra to uncover a bounty: pert, creamy flesh tipped with coral-hued nipples. Fondling and kissing those breasts in the attic had been just a tease. He reached forward to cup her, learn her. He leaned in to bury his face between the mounds, inhaling her scent.

Poppy. Breathe her in.

Neanderthalian? He felt like it. He wanted to pin her down on furs before a fire and rut her like an animal.

Yet at the same time he needed to cherish her. He faced her again. "Poppy . . ."

"Your eyes are ablaze."

As smoke drifted from his skin, he admitted, "Lust is about to overwhelm me, and yet my feelings for you are infinitely stronger." When the visitors had captured him, he'd had no thoughts of self-preservation, only fear for her. Suddenly, he'd become more than himself. Rök had assumed that would happen as he claimed his mate; instead, it'd happened as he'd been about to lose her. "I've never experienced anything like this."

She tenderly cupped his cheek. "Being with your mate is so different?"

"Oh yeah. Not only because you're my fated one." He exhaled a breath. "I just . . . I *like* you, Red. Always have."

"I like you too, Rök." They shared a grin until she slid out of her panties, stupefying him. "If you don't hold back with me, I won't hold back with you."

Transfixed by her lush sex, he rubbed his tongue over a fang.

"This will probably work best if you remove your clothes too. Rök?"

"Huh? Ah! On it." He unbuckled, yanked, and tugged. Stripped before her, that same electrical anticipation before battle hit him—not because his life was on the line but because his future was. This woman was his future. After endless eternities of waiting . . .

Nothing had ever mattered more than what they were about to do. No job. No insurrection. No battle.

"Are you planning to bite me?" she asked.

"Up to you." He'd gone for casual, but his gaze was rapt on her neck and his voice rumbled, his very vocal cords changing as he grew demonic. "It'll mark you forever. You ready for forever?"

She lay back on the divan, a fiery beauty well aware of her effect on him. "Convince me."

"Teasing witch." He moved between her thighs, rolling her nipples till her hips rocked and the scent of her arousal grew undeniable. Then he caressed down her torso, running the backs of his fingers over her mons.

Lids heavy, Poppy let her arms fall over her head, her knees opening wide in invitation.

Quaking from the effort not to fall upon her, he lowered his hand to her sex. His reverent fingers played with her moisture, daubing it on her clit, making everything slick. When he delved one finger inside, the feel of her tight channel threatened to rob him of his new seed.

It struck him: *I could get a pup on her.* "Are you on anything?"

She shook her head, red locks gleaming on the divan. "I

can drink a tea in the morning, and we'll be good."

He was about to give her his seed. Still in disbelief, he worked a second finger inside her sheath, filling her until she gave a throaty moan. Like him, she neared her peak.

"Ah-ah. Don't come till I'm inside you." He thrust his fingers. Spread them inside her. Withdrew them. Thrust them deeper.

She shamelessly met his hand. "I'm ready, Rök!" She was, her body opening for him like a bloom.

"How am I doing so far? Earning forever yet?"

Even as tension built in them both, she joked, "One last part of you I want to test-drive before I sign on the dotted line."

"Then let's get you behind the wheel." He slipped his fingers free and positioned himself in the cradle of her thighs. *This is actually going to happen.* When she nodded, he realized he'd spoken aloud.

Eyes luminous—with arousal—she said, "If you think you can handle it."

For the first time in his long life, he wondered. . . .

SEVENTEEN

Rök looked wild in his lust, a hot, lathered demon rising above her, one who'd waited thirteen centuries for this.

The chandeliers illuminated the changing contours of his face as he turned more demonic. But the harsh planes were just as stunning to her as his fantasy-worthy body—his brawny arms flexing, his torso muscles rippling down to his narrow waist. The crown of his straining cock glistened.

For me.

The prospect of his size and his bite might have given her pause, but she figured both would be as sublime as everything else they'd shared.

Trusting him, she reached up to feather her fingers over the wounds across his rigid chest. He'd earned those injuries fighting her curse. Yet he was also rapidly healing because of her. Already they were connected.

"You are exquisite, mate." He teased her nipples between his fingers, gently plucking them as she arched to follow the sensations. "I'll be fighting off rivals for eternity."

All attitude, she said, "*If* I sign on." But she had. Poppy wasn't just his; Rök had been meant for her too. Fate had it right.

"Have my work cut out for me, then." When the tip of his cock kissed her damp entrance, he hissed in a breath. He fisted the base of his shaft to guide it home. A tilt of his hips . . . nudging, nudging inside her hungry core.

Her eyes widened at the fullness, but she rocked up for more.

"Dark gods, you're hugging the head." As he pressed into her, stretching her, a growl rumbled from his chest. Inch by inch, he fed her his length, sweating from the effort to go slow.

A bead descended from his neck and clung to one chiseled pec. She traced the drop to his nipple, scraping the wet tip with her nail.

Despite his shudder of delight, he grated, "You're testing my control? A demon on the verge of losing it?"

"Yes! Handle it, merc."

He squeezed his eyes closed. When he opened them, he nodded and continued his inexorable claim. As an aura of smoke surrounded them, he grated words in Demonish.

"What did you say?"

"I promised myself to you"—his voice was rough—"even if you aren't yet sold on the idea. And I told you I never want to separate from you again. We do not part, Poppy."

"You're swaying me." With him, her heart was engaged in this act, not just her body, and it was like adding heat to a concoction; now magic would happen as never before. "Keep swaying me."

Once he'd seated himself as deep as she could take him, he nearly forced the air out of her lungs. He stilled, letting her get used to his size. His gaze held hers as he groaned the word: *"You."*

She understood. She gasped her answer: *"You."*

When he ground against her, pleasure radiated throughout her body. Taking a ragged breath, he withdrew and pumped his hips, turning her cry to an abandoned moan.

His expression grew agonized. "Poppy . . . *gods*!" He sheathed himself with a long, steady stroke. And again.

"More, Rök! Don't hold back."

He quickened the rhythm. As he bucked inside her, skin slapped skin and sensation scrambled her mind.

He seized her hips, using his thumb to rub her clit with each thrust. His gray gaze locked on her bouncing breasts, his horns swelling. More smoke rose from his heated skin.

Riding her. Rocking her. Working her slippery bud. With that lost look in his eyes.

Sweat dripped from his forehead to ping one of her aching nipples, more stimulation for a greedy witch. "How're we looking"—he plunged his cock even deeper— "for forever?

"Not yet!" she lied. Sensation melded with emotion, seasoned with magic and fate; she and Rök were one.

Poppy couldn't hold out against such an onslaught. As his hips pistoned, the need for release reached a flash point. Too much. Too much! She squeezed her thighs around his waist, bracing for a climax so strong she almost feared it.

I'll never be the same. Never.

And still, she surrendered, diving headlong into deep water. "Coming for you, demon!" Her vision blurred as she loosed a desperate scream: "RÖK! Yes, yes, *YES*!" Tumbling over the edge, she pulsated around his thick rod until she swam in ecstasy. . . .

Rök didn't want this to end, but he couldn't resist her sultry clench much longer.

He watched enthralled as his shaft emerged wet from her orgasm. *No, don't look there.* But every other sight increased the pressure.

Those quivering breasts. Her panting lips that had sucked him so hungrily. Her lust-glazed eyes. Her pale neck—

"Can't . . . can't hold my seed!" His body was a mass of agony, unequaled in all his battles. The air was redolent with her honey; each inhalation ratcheted up his need.

Between breaths, she said, "You have to hold out . . . I want another! And you still need to mark me."

He gnashed his fangs, about to spend just from the words *mark me.* "Forever?"

She nodded eagerly. "Forever."

He shook his head, his muscles quaking. "I'm too far gone!"

"Think of something else."

"Like bloody what?"

"Desh?"

Rök froze. "You didn't."

"*Did.* Will do it all night!" She laughed, and he felt the vibrations around his shaft. Because he was inside his mate, and she was *happy.*

Peace and need tangled inside him. "By all the gods, you're a weird little witch." But the throbbing in his shaft had relented a touch.

"Soon to be a satisfied one." She cast him a heavy-lidded look. "You may continue."

"Oh, *may* I?"

"Do the piston thing with your hips and get that thumb going again. If I were a strategist like you, I'd bite my mate while she's coming a second time."

"Your parameters . . . are sound." Thumb rubbing, he bucked even harder than before, making her eyes roll back in her head, all thoughts of joking aside.

Another thrust. Another. Giving her what she'd demanded as he fought to hold on.

When her thighs tightened once more—his woman's tell—he grated, "Mine, Poppy. All mine, forever."

"Do it! Mark me *hard*, demon."

"Fuh huh kuhk." Body still working hers, he leaned down to kiss her neck, preparing her for his claim—

She grabbed his horns to steer him! "Now!"

"POPPY!" He sank his fangs into her giving flesh, and a shock wave reverberated through him. *"Uhn!"*

She came from the penetration. He growled against her neck as her fists gripped his horns and her channel milked his cock.

Ungodly pleasure swept him up. He felt as if he floated—becoming one with the smoke inside him—suspended in the space between fire and air.

All his life he'd been smoke searching for fire—nebulous and disconnected. *No longer.* He'd found her at last, his flame. She was his reason for being.

Her mindless cries took him to heights unimagined. Seed climbed. No turning back. *Pressure.*

So much ravaging pressure.

He released his bite to throw back his head, his roar echoing all around them. His hips jerked above her, cock pulsing.

As that pressure gave way to jets of seed, she branded him, connecting him, lighting his way. . . .

Forever.

The demon lay atop her, his heart thundering against hers. Poppy's magic and his smoke mingled in the stillness of the ballroom.

Basking in his warmth, she murmured, "You." *I love you. I need you.* Rök was hers.

Maybe she'd come to this place not only to break a curse but to find him.

He nodded and rasped, "Ah, Red, *you.*"

EIGHTEEN

Hours later, they lay on the dust cover on the floor, spent. Poppy had her head on Rök's chest as he lazily threaded his fingers through her hair.

After indulging in another couple of rounds, they'd shared her apple muffin and some ideas for the future, then they'd set back in.

Eventually she'd begged *no more*, and still he made her come again. They'd broken the divan, so they'd moved to the floor with a vow to buy a stronger one for their new house.

This demon actually had been saving his coin very well. If she desired a mansion near her family with the biggest kitchen they could find, he'd purchase it today.

But all idylls must end. "As much as I'm enjoying this," he said, voice husky from his bellows, "I don't want to be late for the castle's grand opening."

When Poppy leaned up, his attention stole to his mark on her neck, pride and relief filling him. Already her regeneration was healing it, but the mark would remain forever.

"Me neither." Her cheeks were flushed, her eyes bright.

Their lovemaking had chased away her worries, leaving him with a merry witch.

The storm had ended, and moonlight streamed through the windows to bathe her skin as she rose. Watching her don her clothes was nearly as sexy as her stripping them off.

He was about to kiss her again, but the stakes were too high. He rose to dress as well. "Maybe we should have made our way to the foyer and then attacked each other there."

She glanced at her watch. "Moonset's in two hours. Without the visitors dogging our every step, we should be okay."

He didn't understand how she'd quelled her curse, but they would figure out everything together. *We have time.*

Strapping on her satchel, she added, "Besides, we were living in the moment! Would you take back what just happened on that poor piece of furniture? Rest in pieces, divan."

They shared a grin. Fuck, he was going to love life with her. They'd talked about having kids eventually, but for now, she wanted Rök all to herself. He felt the same about her, so she would drink a tea upon their return, and he would use a contraceptive charm going forward. . . .

Hand in hand, they left the ballroom with a last look. This was the place where they'd become *Poppy and Rök*, the mated pair, yet they would never see it again in all their immortal lives.

Outside, they carefully threaded their way back through the maze, taking in the aftereffects of Rök's bruising battle.

Entering the castle once more, they paused long enough to settle on a likely direction—they couldn't exactly retrace their original path—then set off through the endless hallways, turn after turn. Rök still hadn't scented the other explorers, which meant Raven's Murk would keep that secret for now. He and Poppy saw no signs of visitors, as expected, but loud knocks sounded from the direction of the lab.

The creature.

Poppy asked, "You think it knows the castle won't open again for decades?"

"Maybe. But I don't believe it can get loose."

"Good. I can't imagine that thing out in the world."

As they navigated their way through the labyrinthine halls, she checked her watch again, appearing stressed. "I'm reminded of all those horror movie characters who have sex, and it ends up coming back to haunt them. Maybe we *should* have headed to the foyer first. Did we make a fatal mistake?"

"We'll get there before moonset." Giving it a second thought, he said, "Let's leg it, just in case."

They did. With each double back, they picked up the pace even more, until they were sprinting along corridors. Their finish line wasn't just freedom from this place. It was the start of their existence *together*.

They ran for that life . . . reaching the foyer where it'd all begun—with only a quarter of an hour to spare.

Heading to a front window, they gazed out. "No sign of the ghouls," Rök said. "Do you still have an ominous sense?"

Catching her breath, she said, "What I'm feeling for you kind of overwhelms everything, so I don't even know up from down." His arm found its way around her at that. "To be fair, I once experienced foreboding just because Clove had a wicked case of heartburn."

He chuckled. "Fair enough." He noticed Poppy looked excited but also tired. "You must be exhausted." He kept forgetting she was only a hundred. At her age, he'd required sleep every twenty-four hours. She'd fueled curses and fought for her life all night, so maybe he ought not to have ravished her so many times? "My young mate."

She tilted her face up to him. "When you look at me all tender like that, I'm defenseless."

He pressed a lingering kiss to her lips. "Why don't you rest a bit?" He led her over to a nearby settee. "I'll stand watch."

She sat, retrieving the journal from her bag. "What a night." She opened the book, skimming pages.

"Never had a stranger—or better—one." Even so, he was ready for it to end. Rök turned back to the window, hungering for dawn.

As he kept vigil, light effects and breezes made the terrain appear to shift. How differently he viewed this place now that he better understood the tragic history. *The Ending of Everything.* Over his shoulder, he asked, "Anything else interesting in that journal?"

"Most of the pages have blood on them. My sister Sage can clean it up once we get loose. But I did read something strange: *Nightside is real. I found it! All the answers lie in Nightside.* Have you ever heard of that place?"

"Sounds familiar." Hadn't his parents told him about a realm one did not ever want to visit? The answer was on the tip of his tongue when a different kind of light drew his attention to the cemetery. Instead of the coming daybreak, he spied . . . a growing green blaze.

Ghouls had amassed, and not just the wife and kids. Seven more had joined them. A true troop.

The Valkyries kept their numbers in check in populated areas, but out here, nothing had tamped down the swell. As long as that troop stayed away, he and Poppy would be okay—

The green mass started toward the castle. *Fantastic.* One scratch or a mere fang graze spelled doom, and a ghoul's entire reason for being was to infect others.

As they neared, he made out other details. Recognition hit,

and his stomach clenched. Poppy's foreboding had been bang-on. These were no ordinary ghouls.

Trying to sound casual, he said, "So do you think the tracing ban will lift as soon as the door opens?" Even if those ghouls rushed in, Rök might be able to teleport her without a fight.

She glanced up from the journal. "No. I think all the spells will remain. Nothing should change except for the door opening. But you can trace me from the steps outside."

He would need a foot or so of clearance for both of them. If the ghouls charged the door, would he have enough time to strike them down before it closed again? "How long do you think it takes a raven to call four times?"

"It's a big debate on the message boards. A lot of members believe magic must dictate the bird's actions, and now we know"—she held up the journal—"that the wizard used it to call his kids in from play. If I had to guess, I'd say the raven caws every few seconds or so, mimicking the rhythm of a bell tower."

So . . . a handful of seconds? Regardless, Rök couldn't bet their lives on speculation.

He weighed his options.

Scenario one: not enough intel, likely mission failure. *Can't risk her.*

Scenario two: mission failure.

Scenario three: supreme mission failure.

Once he'd exhausted dozens of possibilities, he stared off at his future in disbelief. *Poppy and I aren't making it out alive together.*

"How wild is it that we'll soon lay one more mystery to rest?" she said.

That wasn't all they'd be laying to rest. Or, rather, to unrest.

She began musing aloud where they should get breakfast—"I'm thinking beignets and chicory coffee"—not noticing his tension.

Even as he monitored the threat skulking closer, he treasured her happy chatter. He wanted this taste of normalcy for just a little longer.

After searching for his mate for more than a thousand years, he'd claimed her, and she'd taken control of her curse. For a brief moment, he'd been able to envision their lives together. Talking over meals. Making love. Mercenary gigs as an indomitable team. Halfling pups.

Yes. Enjoy this taste. "So where would you like to live?" he asked, keeping his cool, even as he knew what he'd have to do.

These are my last minutes—as me.

"I'm not picky. As long as you're there, it's home."

His eyes squeezed shut. Her heartfelt words pained him so badly that she might as well have struck him.

Cade had once described what being separated from Holly felt like: a huge hole through the chest that never healed. *Exactly, friend.* Rök wished he could send a message to Cade to watch over Poppy and safeguard her through the Accession.

"Where are you taking me after this, demon? I wouldn't mind freshening up before beignets. Oh! I want to see your new place. Is your shower big enough for two?"

Yes, it is. More delights they would forfeit.

She must've noticed his disquiet. He could all but hear her frown. "Am I overstepping? I mean, you did say you never want to be separated from me again."

He swallowed thickly, not trusting himself to speak.

"Oh, Hecate, are you regretting things?"

He turned to her. "Never. But . . . we have a problem." He gestured to the window.

Poppy shoved the journal into her bag and hurried to his side. Her eyes widened at the sight of the incoming ghouls. "Those are the explorers."

"So they are."

The six fey archers and the rage demon had likely made it to the grand opening—after all, few dangers existed *within* the castle for those who weren't cursed—only to be turned right when freedom was in reach. Had the mother ghoul done it?

"I recognize those tattoos," Poppy said. "That's Truller the Victor. Or it *was*."

"Gotta be honest, I'm not a fan of his glow-up." The legendary demon was now a yellow-eyed monster.

"The ghouls that the Valkyries make sport of are all former humans. Do you think these ghouls retained their strength and speed?"

"I've seen similar ones on distant planes. The fey will still be as quick, the demon as strong. Think super ghouls."

"How were they not found? The best trackers in the Lore searched for them."

"They must've gotten lost in the wilderness. It's some of the most inhospitable terrain this realm has to offer." Or had they crossed over into *another* realm—the one of the undead—only to return now?

"Why didn't Truller teleport home when he was struck?"

"Depending on the strength of the infecting ghoul, the contagion can work quickly." A detail Rök had factored into his calculations. "Truller might have wanted to spare loved ones. But what's brought them back here tonight?"

"Maybe the only two living people for hundreds of miles. Rök, they'll stop at nothing to turn us. What are we going to do?"

"When the door opens, I'll attack. You'll follow, grabbing my back as I trace."

"No, absolutely not."

"I'm going to annihilate them, Poppy. You saw me fight the visitors. Unlike them, these ghouls can be killed."

"There's not a doubt in my mind that you can take them down. But avoiding a single scratch isn't possible." She studied his expression, and her lips parted. "Oh, Hecate, you *know* you're going to get scratched."

"Not saying it won't be risky, but I've faced worse odds for much less upside."

"No! You'll turn." Her eyes went wild. "Think about what you're saying."

He had. "I'm open to ideas, but I've run down all the possibilities." Each scenario ended with one outcome: Rök would become undead.

"You told me noble wouldn't happen again!" Her gaze darted around the foyer. "Use the closet door as a shield, then we barrel forward."

"A demon as strong as Truller will punch the door, breaking it. I'll be holding pieces of wood instead of a sword. If we lose an inch of ground, which we will with an inswing door and Truller shoving, the fey will swarm in behind him faster than we can blink. Then *you* get clawed. Unacceptable mission failure."

"So we let them in and fight them here. You're mated now and will be stronger than ever. I'll fashion some kind of weapon."

"The only way to outpace a fey is to teleport, which I can't do inside this place. And we have no idea when the door will close. I won't risk you based on message board speculation."

Sounding panicked, she said, "What about a trap?"

"Castle's about to open."

"Then we stay here!" She nodded frantically. "You asked me where I want to live? I lied; I *am* picky. I want to live here with you for the next twenty or so years. We can use the time to plan for when the door opens next. Listen to me, Rök, I'm *in love* with this castle. I can't live without it."

She was telling him she loved him. He could play along.

"My heart is a hundred percent committed to this plan to save you, Red. I'll be devoted to it for the rest of my life."

She understood him, expression going soft.

Then it hardened. "Staying here is our only option. Worst case: we're stuck for two decades, a blink of an eye for an immortal. Best case: my sisters will figure out how to open this place."

"And if they can't? What if they come on the next Halloween moon? That same troop might greet them, if it isn't even larger. In the meantime, you would have wasted away to nothing."

"I'm old enough to revive."

"Before I watch you suffer like that, I'd rather be undead." Which was no longer his worst fear. He recalled his bafflement that Cade might choose Holly over the fate of an entire kingdom. Now Rök understood.

I would sacrifice anything *for Poppy.* His life? *Of course.*

"But you'll leave me to watch you turn?"

"There's no other way. This castle isn't safe. Once the lack of food hit, we'd be defenseless. What if that creature gets the door combination right? And if you aren't conscious to mute your curse, the visitors will descend upon us again."

She started to argue more, but he said, "Poppy, there's no special tea here. If I got you pregnant, how would we keep our babe alive? Even if we could feed a child, would you like to raise it here past its teens?"

Her hand dipped to her belly. Oh, the thoughts swirling behind her eyes . . . There was no argument, and she knew it.

"I'll take the hits, love. That's what mates do."

Her gaze glinted. "Remember how we shuddered at the fate of the wizard's family? You'll join them?"

"Use your witchly skills to discover a cure. Concoct something for me to take."

"No witch has ever formulated a ghoul countermeasure, and many have tried!"

"Yeah, but you're *Poppy*. Find some cool plant, and make it work for us."

She grabbed his arms. "Leave me here. If you got a running start and half-traced, they might not land a strike. Work with my sisters to open the castle."

"We don't have time to argue, so I'll make this simple: I vow to the Lore that you and I are both getting out of here, one way or another, once that door opens."

An unbreakable vow. "You didn't."

"*Did*. Will do it forever, witch."

Her bottom lip quivered. Her eyes welled with tears, alight with feeling, and it was gutting him. In a thick voice, she said, "I can't lose you, Rök. We just found each other."

He swallowed, swamped with emotion. But he needed to stay frosty to get her free—

Loud footsteps pounded outside. *What now?* Through the window he spied yet another green creature advancing on the castle, but this one was gargantuan. Must be ten feet tall.

Poppy wiped her eyes and followed his focus. "Great Hecate. I've never seen one that big."

"Neither have I. Not in all my years. Think I know why."

She gasped. "The word *mord* was in the wizard's journal, smudged on each side. He'd seen the pri*mord*ial." The oldest and strongest of its kind. "That ghoul outside is the seed of them all."

Rök whistled low. "The O.G."

She muttered, "The original ghoul? Oh, Rök, don't ever change."

He stifled a wince. He was about to change more than he'd ever imagined. "I bet it turned the previous explorers when they strolled out the door twenty years ago. Talk about a mission hiccup."

"The wizard wrote that the gateway to an undead realm might be in the vicinity. I think he was right. After all, this primordial came from somewhere." True. Most immortal species hailed from distant planes.

As the behemoth stalked closer, those super ghouls darted out of its way, regrouping behind it. Yet then it paused in front of the window. It met Rök's gaze, and he detected . . . a type of *sentience* in its yellow eyes. Extending an arm, it grasped for something with those lethal claws.

New blood, no doubt. And Rök knew it was about to get its wish.

Would turning hurt? *Turning.* Such an innocuous word for *dying.* Yet even as these morbid thoughts raced, he only felt fear for Poppy.

The primordial stomped toward the stairs. Outside the door, it roared with anticipation, yet it didn't try to force its way in.

Did it sense the boundary, or did it somehow . . . *know* about it?

Would Rök know his fate? *Will I know I love Poppy but still be compelled to hurt her?*

Clutching his hand, she said, "This changes everything. Rescind your vow. We stay."

He faced her. "All I have to do is keep you protected long enough for me to trace us."

She looked aghast. "You're not even going to *try* to avoid being scratched?"

He opened his arms to her. "That's not the mission, love."

NINETEEN

One thing Poppy had learned from her years as a mercenary? In a crisis, people revealed themselves.

Rök was revealing himself as exactly what he'd said earlier. A hero of old.

She gazed up at him. He was so stalwart, even as a primordial ghoul—the bogeyman of them all—prowled mere feet away. Despite Rök's revulsion toward undead creatures, he was ready to become one to protect her.

She went into his arms.

Against her hair, he promised, "I'm going to kill them all, Poppy. Even the primordial. Rest easy on that score."

"And you're going to pay the ultimate price." She was tempted to knock him unconscious and drag him into hiding. But even if she managed to drop a statue bust on his head, the blow would just piss him off. "This isn't the way."

"No?" He drew back to face her. "You know me; I'm a demon through and through. Could anything be more demonic than charging horns-first into hell to defend my cherished mate? Poppy, I was fucking *born* for this."

But hadn't she been born to protect him as well? Each scenario they'd discussed assumed Rök bearing the brunt—because she was defenseless.

Out of pouches. Out of luck.

Shock coursed through her. *Is this really happening?* Reality felt dreamlike, a horror movie in slow motion.

He caught her gaze. "Here's the plan. Since I have no idea what the primordial's toxin will do, I'll trace you to Erol's. If I turn quickly, the immortals there will make short work of me. If I have more time, I'll return here. Tell Cade to send my crew on a bug hunt to off me."

"You said you wanted me to cure you!" More tears pricked her eyes.

"I thought better of that plan. What if I attack you? I can handle this fight, but I can't handle the idea of my harming you. Besides, now that you can control your curse, you've got no limitations. This is my Ending of Everything—but it's not yours. If you live on, then every step I've ever taken to get to this point was worth it. I want you to get over me and get on with life. You're young. A Wiccan can move on."

"Fuck you, Rök," she quietly said, tears spilling over. "You're my mate too."

A gust of breath left him. "Yeah?"

She nodded. "You asked me when I knew about you. On our date, I thought: *He's the one.* It's never faded, even when I wished I could hate you."

He leaned down to kiss her damp cheek. "This isn't what I wanted for you." His voice was hoarse. "Had big plans for us, you know? But I screwed up. I should've talked to you. I could've helped you with the curse. You never would've had to come here. Now . . . I'm leaving you."

The question kept repeating: *Really happening?* The ghouls

grew quiet, as if to emphasize the coming moment, the culmination of a thirteen-hundred-year life.

A sob escaped her. She swiped tears, but they kept falling. "I-I will find a way to bring you back. You will come back to me." Unless the brutal immortals at Erol's dispatched him.

Rök tightened his arms around her. "Hey, hey, none of that."

Between sobs, she whispered, "I love you."

"How could you not?"

Hollow laugh.

"For the record, I love you too, Poppy."

I can't lose him. But she couldn't fight for him. Her only seeming ability was to mute curses. Could she use it against ghouls? They hadn't been cursed, at least not magically; their contagion was biological, spread outward from that primordial in a line of tragedy and terror. "You said we were in our very own horror movie. Now you're about to draw the monster."

"Yeah." Rök gazed down at her like he'd never see her again. "When you love something, you protect it."

Exactly what he'd said on their date—what should have been their beginning. Now . . . the end of them.

But she loved him too. Why couldn't *she* protect *him*?

"It's almost time. I'm going to face the door and focus. Stay at my back and follow close." He pressed a kiss to her trembling lips, catching another sob. "Poppy, nothing has ever made me prouder than being your mate." He turned from her and readied his sword with his shoulders squared.

Crying freely, she raised her palm to his back. He tensed, but then leaned into her touch.

Connection.

Can't lose him. She dashed her tears away. Tears had never helped her, but sometimes rage had. When she pictured Rök clawed, bitten, and afflicted, rage boiled up until she choked on it. No. No. *NO.*

Boiling, boiling, her veins burning with it. *Power* boiling?

Shades of her visitors appeared, half-visible and soundless around the perimeter of the large foyer. The worst ones had collected.

Of all the timing. *How dare you, you vile monsters.*

Rök hadn't sensed them yet, had his gaze fixed on the door, all too ready to sacrifice himself.

She tried to access her power and defeat the curse once more, but the visitors didn't budge. Her lips drew back from her teeth as she swept her gaze over them. *I'm going to murder you all. Somehow. Some way.*

Had the razor-gloved maniac winced? Why wouldn't the slasher meet her eyes? He usually loved to cast her killing looks. The dolls craned their heads from her. Even the Horseman's silent steed averted its gaze.

They . . . cowered.

From me?

More than that, they appeared to await something from her.

Willing to try anything, she crooked her finger at Annelise's shadowy form. *Come here. I'll rip your swiveling head right off.*

The blank-eyed doll appeared on her shoulder, hanging out like a ventriloquist's dummy, posing zero threat.

Poppy's jaw dropped.

The doll's telekinesis grew palpable. Instead of struggling against it, Poppy opened herself up to the power. She sensed it entering her own magic arsenal, exponentially more potent than before—as if it were Poppy's inborn gift.

Which, she now supposed, it was.

In the end, when all is lost, clarity is found.

Poppy's ability wasn't to mute curses. Nor was she a source that fueled someone else's hex. She was a conduit between the nightmares of humans and reality. She could conjure their fears, corporealize them, and control them.

Manifesting horror. What a dark, sinister power.

Her lips curved. Perfect for a witch.

She turned her smile to the visitors, who all flinched again—as if she was the horror villain. *I'm* their *nightmare.*

Their queen.

They'd been goading her, testing her boundaries to make her act and take control. *I'd still had more to learn.* But wasn't that always the way?

When she curled her fingers and beckoned them, the visitors solidified around her. They were monstrous. Ominous. *Now they're mine.*

Rök whirled around with widened eyes. "Poppy, don't move!" With Annelise in his sights, he raised his sword, like he was about to swat a lethal bee.

"Demon, wait." As even more visitors took shape, her body began to vibrate. "Something's happening."

Poppy backed from Rök, urging him away from the entry. With each of her steps, the stone floor cracked beneath her vibrating body. "Come. I won't let those ghouls take you from me."

Her words recalled Mariketa's: *If you find your prize . . . don't let them steal it from you.*

Rök had never planned on stealing her prize; he *was* the prize.

Those who thought to steal from a witch didn't live to regret it.

"Poppy, the door's about to open." How confused he must be! "We've got bogeys front and back. Use your power against the visitors, so I can do what I need to."

Her voice was unrecognizable. "That's not the mission, love."

TWENTY

Poppy's hair streamed around her radiant face, and her lavender eyes shone with menace, even as her smile was as brilliant as the coming dawn. Her body vibrated until her steps cracked stone. Looking like a terrifying goddess, she continued to back away from the door.

He couldn't stop his feet from following her. He'd follow her forever. But he needed to defend against the coming blitz—against a primordial and more. "Hey, what are we doing here?" Had she been taken over by these visitors? They were everywhere, more appearing at every second.

Stone grit swirled around Poppy like a cloud of his smoke. "Don't you see, Rök? I *am* the scariest thing in this castle."

CAWWWW! cried the raven.

The front door swung wide.

Rök whirled around as the primordial charged inside with a roar, the others on its heels. "Stay behind me!" He gripped his sword—

Out of the corner of his vision, he spied Poppy wave her arm in sync with the doll on her shoulder.

His jaw slackened when the ghouls' bodies left the floor—the primordial's included. Suspended in the air, they thrashed their limbs, claws whistling with each useless strike.

Rök pivoted to Poppy, thunderstruck. "You're controlling the visitors?"

Slow nod. Moving her hands, Poppy telekinetically turned their foes this way and that, like a ghoulish snow globe.

Mesmerizing to watch, but . . . "We're on a clock, witch."

"Very well." Another wave of Poppy's arm launched the ghouls out of the castle. They howled as they sailed all the way to the distant cemetery. Tombstones cracked like dried mud when they landed, dazed.

She turned to the Horseman. "Do your thing."

Sword raised, he spurred his steed and raced through the doorway. A legion of others followed—scuttling, tumbling, loping after him—like he was a cavalry officer mounting a charge.

Rök could imagine him yelling, *To the cemetery, villains!*

CAWWWW! cried the raven.

"That's the second one, Red. We've got to go."

Poppy's vibrations eased until she was able to walk naturally. When she took Rök's hand and they started into the crowd, the mass of visitors filing out of the castle parted for her like a current around a boulder. Together he and the witch hurried to the door.

He held his breath as they crossed the boundary. *"Free."* Trapped no more, tension flowed from him—until the ghouls recovered to speed back toward the castle.

Poppy's eyes glowed even brighter, and a wall of vampire bats materialized to intercept them, blocking their vision. Gremlins clung to their legs, slowing them for the werewolves and skeletons to attack.

When the witch cricked her neck, aliens tackled Truller,

stabbing him with their tails, treating him like a sword dummy. Green blood spewed.

The Horseman and more aliens targeted the primordial, taking it to the ground. The slasher, the killer clown, and a gang of others joined in.

CAWWWW! cried the raven for the third time.

Should Rök trace Poppy away? He turned to her. "Are you going to kill the primordial?" What would the ramifications be?

Bloodlust in her eyes, she smiled. "Yes. Yes, I think I will."

Glorious witch.

With a flick of her hand, her minions redoubled their frenzied attack. As they mauled the primordial, screams rent the night. "Listen to them." She faced Rök, gaze shimmering. "What music they make."

His grin was part humor, part grim fascination. There he and Poppy stood at the threshold of Raven's Murk, staring at each other as more visitors sprang to life all around them and filed from the castle. "How many are under your control?"

"As many as there are nightmares."

Then her power was colossal. "You saved me, love." Rök had accepted his unspeakable fate. Now . . . his future with Poppy awaited once more.

"Just like you saved me all night. We'll always save each other." She stood on her toes, brimming with magic. "Kiss me."

His gaze slid to the doll still perched on her shoulder.

Poppy told it, "Take care of our pawns." When Annelise turned her head 180 degrees to focus on the action, Poppy teased him, "Is my creepy still cute?"

Nodding helplessly, he claimed her lips as monsters battled monsters and an ancient primordial fought to the death.

Rök tasted her power, as arousing as her fierce attitude. Despite the nightmares surrounding them, he got lost in that kiss.

Taking her mouth . . . promising himself . . . forever . . .

Forever.

Forever.

Dimly, he heard an echoing roar. When she drew back, he blinked to attention. "Poppy?"

"I can sense the scene through the visitors." The primordial's roar abruptly ended. "It's done."

"The other ghouls?"

"A few fled. The mother and kids were the first out. Should we pursue them?" Poppy asked, though her ability must be taking a toll. She was young, and she'd just eliminated the strongest ghoul in all the worlds!

Rök wrapped his arms around her. "Another day."

CAWWWW! cried the raven for the fourth and final time.

The castle door slammed shut.

Then Rök traced his mate away from Raven's Murk, never to return.

Poppy glanced around a rustic cabin filled with technology—monitors, computers, and communications gear. "Where are we? This place looks like a spy expert's command center." Sunlight flooded in through the cabin's windows. Rök must've taken her far from the castle.

He released her. "You're in my secret lair, tucked in the wilds of Iceland."

She waved Annelise away, and the doll vanished. Poppy's new ability would take some getting used to, but after tonight . . . she was a devout fan of the franchise. "Iceland? I thought demons liked warm weather." She didn't remark on the horn-sized gouges marring the walls and the pair of larger holes worn into the floor. Her poor anguished demon!

"Though most of us hanker for hellplanes, some of us see the appeal of snow. As long as there's fire." He crossed to a great hearth and tossed logs in. In moments, flames crackled, and he stood. "I bought this place with you in mind. But then I realized you would want to be close to your family."

"And Newt."

His lips curled. "And Newt. The humping cat."

Grinning, she turned to the nearest window. In one direction, a snow-draped mountain loomed; in the other, an active lava flow meandered by like a river! She gave a laugh. "Let's not be too hasty. This place is amazing."

He joined her. "Witches gather on that snowy peak each year in pilgrimage. Between that and the smoke, I was sold."

"Fire and ice, huh? Kind of like your fighting style."

He inclined his head, but she could tell he was pleased. "Your own fighting style defies description. It was like you commandeered an army. Did you turn the curse back on itself?"

"There was never a curse." She explained how her conduit worked. "Mariketa was right; the answer was in that magic-laden castle." Poppy had just needed several helpings of incentive, seasoned with danger, and fired with a demon. "This ability is so unique and so under my control that I think . . . Rök, I think I'm a *queen*." A mystical practitioner better at a particular skill than anyone else in the Lore.

"The witch queen of Halloween," he said, beaming with pride.

The rightness of that title warmed her. "That's me." *Why nightmares?* she'd wondered. But then, how could some witches control storms? Or animals?

"Just when I thought you couldn't be any sexier." He cupped her face to kiss her.

"Wait." She held up a forefinger. "I need to let my sisters know I'm okay."

"Use my computer." He traced over to log her in. "I'll text Desh and make sure he remembers *not* to return for you."

"Good idea." She removed her bag and emailed a quick note: *You bitches won't believe what happened! Drinks on me! Oh, and Lea, we're gonna throw hands.* As Poppy hit send, she recalled something from the chaotic moments before. "Rök, did you happen to notice anything strange when we were kissing?"

He sent the text, then pocketed his phone. "You'll have to be more specific. When I was about to take your lips, I'm pretty sure pumpkin-head gave me a thumbs-up with his stalk hand."

Good point. "Out of the corner of my eye, I thought I saw . . ." She frowned, then shrugged off her concerns. "Probably a visitor I didn't have a handle on, one bringing up the rear for protection."

"I still can't believe a young witch like you took out a primordial. That victory will give a lot of Loreans hope. It'll certainly worry the Møriør." Their alliance contained several primordials from various species.

"It's about time something did." What a difference a night could make! She kicked back in his chair, steepling her fingers. "So this place is half mine?"

"Everything of mine is, including my merc crew. I'm still hoping you'll be the co-leader."

She rose and sauntered over to him, holding his gaze. "Uh-huh. And what about all those pesky summonings?"

"Soon to be things of the past." He'd just said those words when the edges of his body started to blur. "No. No, no, no!" Though he clearly fought it, he was disappearing. "Poppy, it's . . . happening."

Fatigue and disappointment crashed over her. "You gotta be kidding me. It's like a horror trope."

"One last scare, huh?" He looked gutted, his eyes gray with frustration.

His reaction reminded her of everything they'd overcome to get to this point—every foe they'd battled, every mystery solved, every ability realized. A queen like her would never shrink from a challenge.

She grasped his nape. "With the pact you and I made tonight, I summon you back." Her first demonic summoning! Would it work? "Stay with me, Rök. Heed *me*."

A breathless second passed. . . .

By degrees, his form solidified. The strain left his muscles, and he released a relieved exhalation. "Good save, Red." Brows drawn, he rasped, "Just . . . don't ever let me go."

"I won't." She gazed up at him, her mate for life. "I'll summon you back forever—the swimbo of them all—till everyone in the Lore gets the message."

He leaned into her, as if he couldn't get close enough. "What message?"

"That you're mine."

Nodding, he said simply, *"You."*

She rose up to kiss him, saying against his lips, *"You."*

TWENTY-ONE

The creature

He stared at Raven's Murk in the distance, his prison for what felt like eons. After infinite attempts, he'd finally gotten the maddening combination correct and escaped that lab, with not a moment to spare.

Then he'd seen nightmares that defied explanation, even in the Lore, and had used them as cover to steal away from the castle. One thing he knew for certain: that witch and the demon had no idea what forces they'd unleashed. . . .

An immortal raven—once the wizard's eyes and ears—trailed him from above as he turned from the castle. His stomach cleaved with hunger, his mismatched muscles weak. *Ignore the lack. Wrath feeds you.* Now he would know freedom— and *more.*

Retribution beckoned. Though the wizard had been vicious, the one who'd betrayed him first, putting him into the wizard's clutches, was far worse.

Burning with hatred, he tore into the woods, starving for sustenance but even hungrier for revenge.

CAWWWW!

Stay tuned for the next sizzling
Immortals After Dark installment, coming soon.
The Accession is now in full swing.
ARE YOU READY . . . ?

ABOUT THE AUTHOR

Kresley Cole is the #1 *New York Times* bestselling author of the Immortals After Dark paranormal series, the young adult Arcana Chronicles series, the erotic Game Maker series, and five award-winning historical romances. She lives in Florida with her family and too many pets.

KRESLEY CAN BE FOUND ONLINE AT:

Facebook.com/KresleyCole
Instagram.com/KresleyCole
KresleyCole.com

Made in the USA
Columbia, SC
26 March 2024

33660449R00109